FAITH ALIVE!

FAITH ALIVE!

The Secret of Joyful Living

by

AARON N. MECKEL

Author of *Living Can Be Exciting*

ZONDERVAN PUBLISHING HOUSE
GRAND RAPIDS, MICHIGAN

To the members and friends
of the
First Congregational Church
of
St. Petersburg, Florida,
whom it has been my privilege
to serve as pastor
for seventeen years.

I thank my God upon every
remembrance of you!
Philippians 1:3

FOREWORD

As this volume goes to press, world events are very much in flux. Witness Viet Nam, Santo Domingo, etc.! Surely history moves at a frightening pace in these apocryphal times.

And yet, it is comforting to remember that, in such times, there are, for the Christian, the "things that remain," and the

"truths that wake to perish never!" (Wordsworth)

I have sought to state some of them in the pages that follow. As to whether or not I have succeeded, I can only crave the indulgence of the reader.

My thanks are due to so many, only a few of whom space permits mention: My wife, Lillian, who read the manuscript, made pertinent suggestions, and above all else, gave encouragement. My efficient and faithful secretary, Emma Erikson, who typed and revised the manuscript. To my friends at Zondervan Publishing House, who proved so patient and helpful. And last, but not least, to the large and cosmopolitan congregations, who not only listened to the Word as God sought to impart it through His servant, but seek to live and share it.

May some word written here be the means of encouraging and inspiring souls in the Upward Way! This is my hope — and my prayer.

Aaron N. Meckel

St. Petersburg, Florida

CONTENTS

FAITH ALIVE!

1 THAT YOUR FAITH SHOULD STAND!

"That your faith should not stand in the wisdom of men but in the power of God."

(*I Corinthians* 2:5)

IN THE DESPERATE need that faces us in this day, all of us are in need of a faith that will not collapse — a faith that can stand before the blandishments of evil; before the hard knocks and trials of life; before the probings of the clever secular mind of our day. And that precisely is what the Christian faith is: a faith which under God stands on its own feet. The human mind, however clever, is ultimately undependable. The wisdom God has given us in Christ stands fast forever.

When it comes to faith, many people seem unsure of themselves. A brilliant theologian expresses amazement at the number of professionally engaged religious leaders, who are at loose ends as to what they believe. They have a metaphysic for the head, but not a life-giving faith for their hearts.

Now when I speak of a sure faith, I do not mean a theologically cocksure faith — one with all the findings in. I do not mean a religion that is creedally spun out to perfection, but only precariously held.

11

There are depths in the Christian faith which no human mind can ever plumb.

A woman convalescing from a severe illness in a hospital said to me recently, "I will have to do some real 'positive thinking.'" To which I could only reply, "Remember now, not just 'positive' but Christian thinking!"

This is the kind of thinking Paul, the great apostle, was talking about in the mighty second chapter of I Corinthians. At Athens he faced the skeptics of the day. Their religion was something to argue about, a random speculation, a philosophy conjured up by the human mind. But Paul looks them all straight in the eye, and tells them of a "central, funded, founded faith" — one with a Cross, a Resurrection, and a Pentecost at the heart of it. He is frank to tell the Corinthian Christians that he did not come to them with cleverness of speech or wisdom. Rather did he come to declare a testimony and to proclaim a faith. The great sentences of the epistle sound like so many sledge-hammer blows. Just listen:

> For I determined not to know any thing among you, save Jesus Christ and him crucified. And I was with you in weakness, and in fear, and in much trembling. And my speech and my preaching was . . . in demonstration of the Spirit and of power: that your faith should not stand in the wisdom of men, but in the power of God (I Corinthians 2:1-5).

There you have the gist of it. The Christian faith is a *definitely revealed faith,* grounded in the order of event and experience. It descends from Above. Its truth must be realized from within. In a word, it is Within-ness based on Beyond-ness!

A clergyman friend of mine recently gave me his experience. After reading all the available books on the Christian religion he could lay his hands on, and summing up all the arguments, he still was not sure. He finally realized that what was required was the full and total commitment of himself, mind, body and soul, on the Altar of Christian faith and service. Thereupon he received the seal of the Holy Spirit. His faith came alive.

Suppose then, that we look in a few directions in which we can find our Christian faith confirmed and strengthened. Many who read these words will also be saying in the words of the hymn, "Lord, give me such a faith as this!" And thanks be unto God, this faith may be ours.

First of all, let us look at the hungers and longings of our own hearts. None of us are complete in ourselves. We are complete only within the revelation of God in Christ. Well did St. Paul say, "And ye are complete in him" (Colossians 2:10). We are creatures born for a revelation. As Phillips Brooks once said, "Jesus Christ and the human heart are made for each other." Pascal held that the heart is incurably religious, and has reasons of its own the intellect can never know. Our wise Christian forefathers wrote it into their catechism, that man's chief end is to glorify God and enjoy Him forever!

Now, what we have in the New Testament is not a people with speculative ideas *about* God. What we see is, rather, a people rooted and grounded in a saving experience of God's love in Christ. This is what Paul is saying to us across the ages, "I know whom I have believed." In other words, the Christian faith is not a What, but a Whom! It is something intensely personal.

In his interesting book, *God's New Age*, Dr. Nels F. S. Ferré speaks of modern man's difficulty in acknowledging the reality of God. By way of illustration he relates the anecdote of three baseball umpires who were arguing. The first said, "I call balls and strikes exactly the way they come." He was an objectivist. The second said, "But I cannot do that. I call them balls and strikes, just the way I see them."

He was a subjectivist. But the third umpire had an idea all his own. He declared, "They are neither balls nor strikes until I call them." He was an existentialist! Modern man, says Ferré, is like the last umpire. He has to call all life's pitches. He has become so man-centered at the depths of himself, that he has forgotten how to really say, "Our Father, Who art in Heaven!"

Those who have read the life of St. Teresa will recall what a struggle she had in seeking to be sure of God. An acquaintance of hers, a monk, finally suggested that she stop looking outside of herself and look within. She would find God there — and she did. In fact, she found Him as she knelt at the Cross in repentance and faith. And our Lord Jesus Christ Himself, would remind us that, "The kingdom of God is within you" (Luke 17:21).

What we are saying is that, while a viable faith is not lodged within the wisdom of man, it nevertheless begins with man's deepest and innermost longings to root himself in something beyond himself. After all, we could not seek God unless He had first sought us.

The Christian also looks to a *Book*, the Holy Bible, with its unfolding of a divine and unique history, for assurance.

> We search the world for wisdom
> And come back laden from our quest,
> To find that all the sages said,
> Is in the Book our mothers read!
> —*John Greenleaf Whittier*

Henry Drummond, famous scientist and Christian of a generation ago, found himself getting away from the fundamentals of Christian faith while at school. "I must get back to the Bible," he said, "for I cannot stand this uncertainty."

Many of us are making the same discovery in these unsettling times. We are not asked to consult our Bible for proof texts to support and prop up some personal bias we may have. We are to read it to get the divine point of view, to hear what God has to say about Himself, to receive the cummulative evidence of the Old and New Testaments. As we read, we become aware of a Creator-God who speaks in the events of history, and above all in the supreme events of the life and death and resurrection of His Son. Believe me, the Bible is an anvil which has worn out many hammers! Many of us are finding this to be true in our own experience.

The late William Lyons Phelps of Yale used to say that if he had to choose between the simple teachings of the Old and New Testaments and modern secular education, it would not take him long to decide. Our Christian forefathers saw to it that the central core of our Christian-democratic heritage was dug and quarried out of the Holy Scriptures. Again, according to William Lyons Phelps, no one can be educated in the true sense of the word, apart from the knowledge and teaching of the Holy Bible.

There is a well-known story about a Negro preacher who was presented a book on the higher criticism so-called, by a well-meaning friend. Not long afterward his friend approached him with the question, "How did you like the new book?" The Negro preacher in his naive but sane simplicity replied, pointing to his much loved Bible, "This Book sure do throw a lot of light on that book of yours, don't it?"

I would suggest that if you wish to firm up the foundations of your faith, you look not only to the needs and longings of your own heart, but to the great Book of books, which bears the written revelation of God.

Another source from which we can draw help is, of course, the inspiring fellowship of the Christian Church.

The word *brethren* runs like a motif all through the New Testament. Christianity is never a solo flight into the stratosphere above. It is togetherness in Christ, turned toward great ends. This inspired Christian fellowship began at the empty tomb of Jesus on that first Easter Day, and was reborn and crystallized on the day of Pentecost. There and then, the Church became the New Israel of God, rooted in the unquenchable hope and truth of which the Bible speaks.

The life of her Lord is in the Church, and fellowship within her is a foretaste of heaven itself. No illusion could ever have kept the Christian fellowship alive through almost twenty centuries of history. Within this fellowship the Gospel is re-enacted, and miracles of redemption and healing are constantly taking place.

There are times when, if I feel burdened and alone with my own thoughts and cares, I may be tempted to despair or doubt. These doubts and despairs, however, are invariably dispelled as I find myself in the company of my fellow Christians on the Lord's Day, worshiping God the Father, and lifting up the risen Christ. As I join in the great hymns of the Church and unite in her prayers, I find myself strong again. As I recommit myself to the task of bringing God's Kingdom on earth, a sense of significance comes back into my life.

An elderly deaf man, a devout Christian, was once asked why he came to church when he could not hear a word that was spoken. The questioner received the forthright reply, "Why do I go to church? Because I believe in the communion of saints!" It is always thrilling to remember the promise of Jesus, that wherever two or three are gathered together in His Name, He would be in their midst.

While attending the World's Fair in Brussels, Belgium, a few years ago, my wife and I had the rare experience of worshiping at the religious pavilion one noon hour. People were gathered together from almost every nation under the sun. Only occasionally did a recognizable word break through to us. And yet we were all one in Christ Jesus. We shared in a common Spirit and rejoiced in a common hope! In the words of St. Paul, we were baptized into one Spirit. It was an experience long to be remembered.

This sense of rich, vitalizing fellowship in the Spirit needs to be recaptured in our day. John Wesley, in his *Journal*, tells of attending services at Tolbooth Kirk, an old Episcopal chapel in Edinburgh. It seems the people had lost the sense of the presence of the Living Christ. Here is his *Journal* entry for Sunday, May 23, 1784: "They have lost their glorying; they talked, the moment Service was done, as if they had been in London!"

Let me suggest that, if you have lost your "glorying," you actively share again in the work and worship of a vital and living Christian fellowship. If your faith is to stand, it must be rooted in the fellowship of Christ's believing people. You must belong!

Ultimately, however, if our faith is to stand in the power of God, we must maintain it in relationship to a *Person* — none other than the Lord Jesus Christ Himself. "We are made wise unto salvation through faith which is in Christ Jesus" (II Timothy 3:15). It is He whom God has made both Lord and Christ. In this at least, the noted theologian, Karl Barth, is right — that, in the last instance, God addresses His truth to us in a Life.

We are not speaking now just of the Christ of history, although certainly He appears there like some Himalayan peak. We are thinking primarily of the living, risen, personally experienced Christ of faith. This experience must be gathered up, livingly, into the heart of the believer.

Let me say, for the sake of some who may be struggling with doubts, that this is where I myself have had to come out. We get into trouble, intellectually speaking, when it comes to our *ideas* about God, Christ, and the other distinctives of the Christian creed. Phillips Brooks once said that a man can repeat the Apostles' Creed most eloquently, and yet be an atheist at heart. What we are talking about, therefore, is far more than bare intellectual assent to the content of a creed. We must dare to go deeper in life-giving faith by means of daily personal, existential commitment to Christ Himself. Only in Him are we sure. We must be able to say with Lord Tennyson:

> A warmth within the breast would melt
> The freezing reason's colder part,
> And like a man in wrath, the heart
> Stood up and answered "I have felt."

There is no substitute for personal experience. Read these words written by the most superb of all Christians, the Apostle Paul: "But we have the mind of Christ!" (I Corinthians 2:16). That is a good place for any of us to come out, if not indeed, to begin.

In his autobiography, *Surprised by Joy,* the British writer, C. S. Lewis, makes an interesting confession. He tells us that what he found within himself, as he began to sense the mind of Christ, was not at all pleasant. He discovered a whole pack of lusts in his heart, coupled with a lot of brilliant ideas about God! Finally, at the point where he knelt and unreservedly committed himself to God, the Great Pursuer moved in and took possession. Then indeed he was "surprised by joy."

To this experience of the brilliant Englishman, let me add the testimony of Dr. A. J. Cronin in his autobiography, *Adventures in Two Worlds.* After many years of straining and pushing in his professional medical career, he found himself still spiritually empty. Something was missing in his life. He had forgotten God. Here and there he saw glimmerings of the Christian life in the devoted and dedicated personalities of others, including a humble nurse. What he finally found, and what spiritually revolutionized and settled his life, he expresses in the following words: "I have handed myself over to God, body and soul. It is this surrender, total, unquestioning, in complete and absolute humility, which is the true essential of belief."

2 THE LOST ART OF WINNING SOULS

"Go home to your friends, and tell them how much the Lord has done for you, and how he has had mercy on you."   (*Mark* 5:19, RSV)

LET ME BEGIN this chapter by relating an incident out of the life of the late Merton S. Rice of Detroit. During one of his first pastorates he made the companionship of a man with whom he often went on fishing trips. On these trips they would enter into discussion on a lot of subjects — politics, world events, etc. One subject alone was never brought up — that of the Christian life, and the need of surrender to Christ.

Years passed, and in time the young preacher was succeeded by another who promptly pressed home upon this man the claims of the Gospel. But when confronted with the imperial demands of Christ he replied that the matter could not be very important. "If it had been important," said he, "surely Mr. Rice would have mentioned it. During all the years I knew him he never once mentioned the matter." With a great deal of embarrassment, said Dr. Rice, he found himself going back to his former pastorate and friend, to make amends for his tragic neglect. Said the great soul winner of later years, "We must make our friendships Christian!" The Chief of Police in an Indiana city, looking at the tragic wrecks brought to his attention, was overheard to say, "The saving of souls is rapidly becoming a *lost art* in our generation."

We had better allow that accusation to sink deeply into our minds. A lost art, is it? The outstanding "liberal" preacher of our generation, not long before his retirement from the active ministry, stated in a sermon that, were someone to become soundly converted in some of our churches, we would actually be embarrassed and not know what to do with him. Has the Church lost her first love? Surely the first task of the Christian Church is that of evangelism.

Turn to the Bible and read the fifth chapter of St. Mark's gospel. You will read how Jesus met with a man who was possessed by an unclean spirit and was hidden among the tombs. Thinking that the Lord had come to torment him, he cried out in fear. When Jesus asked him his name he could only reply, "My name is Legion, because there are so many of us." Thereupon the Lord Christ performs a great miracle, surely one of the greatest in the gospel records. With a word, He frees this man from the false grip of sin and fear, and fuses him into a composite soul. He grants him the gift of true manhood and selfhood.

The gratitude of the demoniac is revealed in the fact that he wants to accompany Jesus on His journeys, and to leave his self-centered fellow-townsmen, who after all cared nothing about him. He begs Jesus that he might be with Him. Now, notice the reply that Jesus makes to this man. He is to begin right where he is to be a witness to the healing and redemptive power of his Lord: "Go home to your friends, and tell them how much the Lord has done for you, and how he has had mercy on you." And the result of this man's witnessing? "And he went away and began to proclaim in the Ten Towns how much Jesus had done for him; and all men marveled" (Mark 5:19, 20). He told the story of his redemption so effectively, so fervently, so joyfully, that he revolutionized that whole region! Men were turned to Christ through his witness.

It is high time that we reread our New Testament, and lay fresh hold on this art of bearing effective Christian witness, lest it become a lost art.

Here now are two rather obvious propositions and the inferences that follow from them.

To begin with, the Church grew and became great as believers witnessed to their Lord. The first Christians beheld in their Master a mighty magnet. They lifted Him up in word and deed that He might draw men unto Himself.

As we read again the original documents of our faith, we are convinced that the overall object of those first disciples was not to build a pretentious church, or to pad membership rolls, or to cultivate social or cultural influence in the community. No. Their consuming ambition was to share a life they had found in Jesus Christ. They were on fire to bear witness to One who had redeemed them from the dregs of sin and unbelief. Thus did the Church grow!

And how amazingly simple the method of Jesus! What a wonder that we have lost it! He took twelve men very much like ourselves, lived His way into their lives, filled them to overflowing with this love and concern for others, and then sent them out saying, "Ye are My witnesses." They in turn passed the torch of witness to others, until a great fire was kindled. We read in Acts that those first disciples went everywhere, proclaiming Jesus and the Resurrection, and that the Lord added daily to the Church such as were saved. So did the Church grow! Why, then, has the winning of souls become a lost art in our time? How is it that what the great preacher John Henry Jowett called "a passion for souls" has so much lost its hold on us?

Have we so professionalized our witness that we have

forgotten that Christianity first burst upon the world as a lay apostolate? Can we no longer say with William Carey, "My business is to be a Christian; I cobble shoes for a living"? Perhaps the rather stinging words of Dwight Lyman Moody apply to many of us: "I wouldn't give a dime for that church where the minister does all the preaching, and the praying, and the visiting." Have we surrendered the task of Christian witness over to professional men whom we call our ministers, and who are to do it for us? Or perhaps we have become so obsessed with peripheral and incidental matters — social reform in the large, the raising of large budgets, the whirl of social organizations — that we have lost sight of our primary task. Has the Church ceased to be a revolutionary organism of the Spirit and dwindled into a mass of revolving machinery?

One is led to wonder about that, when he sees the religious cults and sects of the day capitalizing on our lukewarmness. Just take a look at the Jehovah's Witnesses on the streets of our cities, offering their literature to the passerby with a smile.

Not long ago in our church here in St. Petersburg, Florida, an usher came to me as I was preparing to go into the morning service. He said he had been handed a very urgent message for me, and that I was to be sure to read it before going into the pulpit. The message turned out to be propaganda printed and distributed by the Jehovah's Witnesses. This particular Witness wanted to intercept the preacher before he went in to his pulpit. Perhaps he even thought I might be converted to his view of things by taking a look at his literature! Of course I was sorry to disappoint him! But I could not help but admire his intense zeal.

Or pause to think of the religion of Mormonism, the Church of the Latter-Day Saints, as it is commonly called. A minister friend in another state says that whenever a

Mormon family moves into his community, you can feel its missionary fervor for five miles in every direction. Yes, let it be said that when the Congregationalists, the Methodists, the Baptists, the Presbyterians, and the other churches no longer ply their evangelistic witness, then the sects and the cults take it up.

I am also amazed at the fervor and urgency with which the world of business carries on its trade. Just stop and look at the billboards that you pass driving down your street every day, all urging you to buy products of every kind. Sometimes I think that even the Fuller Brush man can teach me to be a better witness!

A Christian layworker was driving in the country when he overheard the radio announcer extolling the merits of a certain product. With what urgency and attractiveness the appeal was made. The children in the home would not be healthy nor would the home be happy without this particular product! My friend said that when his interest was fanned to high flame, he listened carefully for the name of the product. Out it came from the lips of the announcer: "Supersuds!" My friend commented: "Why is it that the average one of us is more enthused about selling automobiles, radios, life insurance, houses, and what not, than he is in communicating the Christian religion?"

Even as the early Christians were driven abroad by persecution, they witnessed to the Lord of life. Persecuted but witnessing! When the Church was great, the winning of souls to Christ was a consummate art.

The second proposition stems from the first. The Church will again become a great power in our modern society as we rededicate ourselves to this lost art of winning souls. Think again of the man whom Jesus healed. No longer did he remain among the tombs. Out he goes, all through his neighborhood and region, proclaiming the glory and the power of the Lord who had delivered him. So much so that all men marveled: "they were all simply amazed" (Mark 5:20, Phillips translation).

A friend of mine, a live Christian layman, told me of spending a weekend in a strange city. While there he visited two churches. The first was disappointingly cold in spirit. There was a noticeable lack of communication — of God with man, and man with man — in that service. By way of contrast, he tells of his experience in another church in that same city, on Sunday evening. The atmosphere of the church was fairly charged with the spirit of a loving concern and friendship. Not noise, mind you, but spiritual intensity and awareness. The sermon was tucked close around the needs of the people. Were he ever to move to that city, he said, he would make it a point to attend that church, and join it.

Now what marked the difference between those two churches? Could not the answer be put thus: In the one church there was a genuine interest in persons as persons; in the other, the people were just automatons, listeners, so many bodies occupying pews.

I never cease to thrill at the spiritual possibilities wrapped up in a service of worship, where both pastor and congregation are on fire with the Christian message. What a Pentecost there could be! If now, someone who reads these words asks, "What are the necessary qualifications for the bearing of an effective Christian witness?" let me mention these few:

(1) First of all, you must have a story of your own to tell.

> Thy soul must overflow
> If thou another soul wouldst reach.
> It takes the overflowing part
> To give the lips full speech.
> —*Horatius Bonar*

People must see the evidence of the working power of God in your life. Talk about yourself, and you become an insufferable bore. Go and tell another what Jesus Christ has done for you, and you become an irresistible magnet.

The late President Woodrow Wilson, himself a son of a Presbyterian minister, once told of occupying a chair next to Dwight Lyman Moody in a barber shop. Moody plied the men about him with questions concerning their personal lives. Occasionally he would ask them about the welfare of their souls. While Moody was there men talked in undertones. Most of them did not know his name; they only knew that something, or someone, had elevated their thought. "I felt," said Woodrow Wilson, "that I left that place as I should have left a house of worship."[1] In a day when the communists and secularists are shrilling out their wares, we must bear our Christian witness more effectively.

(2) Be assured also that love counts for much more than argument in bearing your witness. People are loved rather than argued into the Kingdom of God. During one of the evangelistic tours of Moody and Sankey in England, Moody approached a student in one of the universities. Here is the up-shot of it: Mr. Moody "looked at me . . . and asked me if I would take Christ now. I could not speak, but my heart said, Yes."[2] Oh, for a spirit of winsomeness and love in our lives! For lack of it, our actions repel people, and keep them from our Christian churches. In the unforgettable words of Fanny Crosby:

> Down in the human heart, crushed by the tempter,
> Feelings lie buried that grace can restore.
> Touched by a loving heart, quickened by kindness,
> Chords that are broken will vibrate once more.

There comes to mind the prayer list that my pastor father used to keep. He would record the names of any

[1] J. C. Pollock, *Moody* (New York: The Macmillan Company, 1963), pp. 302, 303.
[2] *Ibid.*, p. 124.

of his flock who might be sick or discouraged or bereaved. Oftentimes on his knees — at family prayers — he would mention them before God, one by one. It is high time that we are putting our prayer lists to work again in the church. I believe with all my heart in the great enterprise of foreign missions — the saving of souls at a distance. But what of the heathen and pagan right in our midst? Evangelism, like charity, might well begin at home. There are literally thousands of persons in our average American community who are unaffiliated with any church. Who is to go out and bring them in if not we? Said Jesus: "Those who are well do not need a physician. The Son of Man has come to seek and to save the lost."

(3) Finally, let us realize that the winning of souls for the Master is our personal task, and that the way to learn is just to begin. Dwight L. Moody once said to a hesitant Christian worker, "You ask the 'how' of it? Start right where you are. The main thing is to begin."

But someone says, "I do not have youth and health and strength. I must leave to others the task of evangelism." My friend, are you saying that there is nothing that you can do? Then let me relate this instance out of the life of Dr. Alexander Maclaren.

Noting a famous skeptic in his congregation one Sunday, Dr. Maclaren talked to him afterward and promised that, if the skeptic would attend the church for four consecutive Sundays, he would endeavor to present the main tenets of the Christian faith. If at the end of that time this man desired to unite with the church, he would be glad to welcome him.

The great preacher was overjoyed to note the eager manner in which the skeptic listened to his presentations, and delighted, when on the fourth Sunday, he presented himself for admission into the church. He even went so far as to inquire which of the four sermons was most instrumental in bringing him to his decision. Imagine his amazement at this reply: "Your sermons, Sir, were helpful, but they were not what finally persuaded me to make my decision." He was leaving the church, he stated, on a cold winter Sunday, when he noticed an elderly woman with a glowing face making her way with difficulty on the icy walks. He stepped up and offered to help her. As they walked along together, she looked up into his troubled countenance and said, "I wonder if you know my Saviour, Jesus Christ. He is everything in the world to me. I would like you to know Him too." Said the former skeptic, "The remark of that little Christian saint sent me home, where, on my knees, I found Christ for myself, and admitted the Holy Spirit into the depths of my heart. Then and there I resolved to be His disciple and a member of His believing fellowship. That is why I am here."

You see it was not so much the persuasive eloquence of the great preacher as the simple testimony of a little handicapped saint that won that man for the Christian cause.

"Go home to your friends," said Jesus, "and tell them how much the Lord has done for you." And how well he did it!

In the end, it will not be so much the worldly honors you have won, or the offices you have held in the church that will bring you deepest satisfaction. It will be the souls who, through your loving concern and interest, were led into the Christian life that will constitute the jewels and gems in your crown!

3 HOW LONG IS YOUR SHADOW?

"... that at the least the shadow of Peter passing by might overshadow some of them."

(*Acts* 5:15)

HORACE BUSHNELL, renowned preacher of yesterday, once gave a sermon he entitled "The Power of Unconscious Influence." This sermon held that each of us carries around with him a kind of personal aura which goes out to influence the lives of others, either for good or ill. This, said the preacher, is the power of unconscious influence. It is a subtle infection or contagion that emanates from us as surely as does fragrance from a rose. I recall some quaint lines by Robert Louis Stevenson I learned as a boy:

> I have a little shadow
> That goes in and out with me.
> And what can be the use of him
> Is more than I can see.

In the fifth chapter of the Acts of the Apostles we learn of the power of a shadow, a far-reaching one. That early Christian Church was a mighty Church! Many signs and wonders happened among the people through the ministry of the apostles. Here were men and women whose lives reflected the power and the presence of Christ. They possessed a contagion which was irresistible. Believers were added to the Lord daily. The sick and the afflicted were laid out on the streets on beds and couches in case one of the apostles should be going by.

Peter in particular must have had a powerful, contagious personality. When people learned that Peter was going to pass their way, they laid their sick ones on beds and couches, so that "the shadow of Peter passing by might overshadow some of them" (Acts 5:15).

Just pause a moment to think of what this means. This was the Peter who had once denied his Master, but was forgiven and redeemed by the shore of Tiberias. God made a failure into a triumph, a nobody into a somebody. The former denier is now prince of the apostles. At Pentecost he preached such a mighty sermon that thousands were added to the Church. In fact, he so reflected the authentic spirit of the crucified and risen Christ that even his shadow healed.

What a man, and what a religion! The shadow of Peter passing by reaches out in blessing and healing to the sick and suffering by the wayside!

Some rather embarrassing questions might be asked at this point. Is there a power of unconscious influence going out from us, to bless the lives of others? Recall what Emerson said: "What you are, speaks so loud I cannot hear what you say." The modern Christian is inclined to be "gabby" and that is about all. Just stop and count out the number of people you know who possess this power of unconscious spiritual influence. You will find them to be few. As Peter walked by on the scorching hot streets of Jerusalem, no herald proclaimed his arrival. There was no publicity agent around taking pictures. What could be more quiet and unpretentious than a shadow! But in the case of Peter and the other disciples, the shadow was far reaching in its healing power.

Suppose we summon the courage to ask a few, frank questions:

1. How far reaching is your shadow when it comes to lifting up the saving power of Jesus Christ from day to day? Are people just the same after meeting you, or is there an inspiration about you that lifts them upward and Christ-ward?

Years ago an Englishman named L. P. Jacks wrote a book he entitled *The Lost Radiance of Religion.* The great tragedy that has befallen modern Christianity, said the author, is its lack of spiritual pervasiveness. It is short on spiritual contagion. It is lusterless and possesses no cutting edge. I wonder, are a lot of our lives like that? Or can we sincerely say with Dr. E. Stanley Jones, "I want to live the kind of life that says to others, 'I commend unto you my Saviour.'"

One of Robert Browning's most beautiful poems is the one he entitled "Pippa Passes." It is the account of a humble little worker in a silk mill who goes singing through her one-day holiday. As she walks along the streets of her drab mill town, she unconsciously radiates joy and good will. The best part of it is that she herself is not aware of her influence on others. She doesn't preach at them. She doesn't even know that anyone is listening. But as she sings, she casts her healing shadow over the troubled lives of people in the houses she passes:

> The year's at the Spring
> And day's at the morn;
> Morning's at seven
> The hillside's dew-pearled!
>
> The lark's on the wing
> The snail's on the thorn;
> God's in His heaven
> All's right with the world.

Talk about the power of unconscious influence — there you have it. It doesn't announce itself. It is utterly unheralded. It just sings.

If you have caught up the saving spirit of Christ in your life, you will not need to preach formal sermons. You will not even have to tell others. They will know. Over the door of a Y.M.C.A. building were written the words, "Be careful what kind of life you live. You may be the only Bible some people read."

2. Again, how long is your shadow when it comes to communicating the spirit of genuine comfort and solace to lives that may be needing it? When Dr. Theodore Parker was asked by a young seminarian what message to preach, he replied, "Preach to broken hearts."

I know how clumsy and awkward we often are when it comes to the fine art of extending comfort. The prophet Isaiah beautifully describes the ability to go out of yourself and enter helpfully into the lives of others. He speaks of the shadow of a mighty rock in a weary land (Isaiah 2:2). Try and picture the scene. The weary pilgrim, plodding along in the desert heat, sees a huge rock in the distance. When he arrives, he sits down; nearby is a spring where he can assuage his thirst. Soon he is refreshed and continues on his long desert march. Isn't that what we should be to others, and isn't that what we should like others to be to us in our time of need? "The shadow of Peter passing by" — how sorely that is needed in the modern shuffle of life.

Early in my ministry I memorized the words of a poem by Anna E. Hamilton. This poem has been a great inspiration to me through the years:

> Ask God to give thee skill
>   In comfort's art,
> That thou may'st consecrated be
>   And set apart
> Unto a life of sympathy,

For heavy is the weight of ill
    In every heart;
And comforters are ·needed much
    Of Christlike touch.

Dr. William S. Reid, a radiant Christian physician, relates an experience at a local hospital in his Texas community. As he was leaving the hospital one day, he met a minister friend who looked very troubled. He learned that this minister's little boy was ill in the hospital and was hardly given a fighting chance to recover. The physician offered to go with the father to see the boy, although he was not the physician on the case. After making a routine check-up, he turned to his minister friend and said: "I am not a minister, but I would be happy to pray with you for the healing of your boy." At the conclusion of the prayer, says Dr. Reid, his friend wiped a tear from his eyes and said a very significant thing: "You know, one of the difficult things about being in the professional ministry is that you and your family do not have a pastor to turn to in time of crisis."

I myself had hardly graduated from theological school and gone to my first church, when I learned a lasting lesson. A business woman of middle years, a faithful member of our church, faced serious surgery. She was not at all demonstrative in her expression of religion. She was a good, faithful plodder, one of the many people who make the Christian ministry worth while. "I am willing," said she, "to have this operation providing my pastor will stand by and pray for me."

Not many days afterward, I found myself in a great hospital, at an early hour of the morning standing at the bedside of this woman, offering spiritual consolation. I assured her that I would pray for her during the time she was in surgery, as well as for those who ministered to her.

Through the skill of a good surgeon and the love of God the patient made a fine recovery.

The point I wish above all to stress is that I discovered the spiritual meaning of the word "shadow." We never know what our lives may mean to someone else. We must be able so to go out of ourselves that we may enter helpfully into the lives of others. Recall how George Eliot once expressed it:

> May I reach
> That purest heaven — be to other souls
> The cup of strength in some great agony,
> Enkindle generous ardor, feed pure love,
> Beget the smiles that have no cruelty —
> Be the sweet presence of a good diffused,
> And in diffusion even more intense.
> So shall I join the choir invisible
> Whose music is the gladness of the world!

We have discussed the power of a shadow in lifting up the saving power of Christ, as well as the ability to enter sympathetically and helpfully into the lives of others. Let us ask one more question: How long is your shadow when it comes to the practice of Christian stewardship?

Sometimes I think the question that will be asked of us by the Great Judge will not be "Were you a member of a church?" or "How often did you go to church?" or any such routine matters, important as they may be. He will simply ask us to give an account of our Christian stewardship. Is our religion a little cozy, parochial affair, content in its provincialism, blind to the gaping wounds of humankind? Have we, through the grace of God, shed the prejudices and hatreds which hinder the coming of the Kingdom of God in our day? Can we see the potential Christ in every man's heart, regardless of color, race, creed, or nationality? The thing that stands most in the way of the coming of God's Kingdom in our day is the prejudice and blindness we may still harbor in our hearts. While at church we have often repeated the words, "Thy Kingdom come, Thy will be done, on earth as it is in heaven," only, alas, to go out and misrepresent them. We have read in our Bibles the words of Jesus' Great Commission to make disciples of all men and of all nations. But we have not really obeyed them.

We find this spirit of Christian world concern in the lives of truly great persons. They make us ashamed of ourselves. They lift us out of our littleness. Some of you have read the book, *September Monkey*, written by the famous Korean Christian, Mrs. Induk Pahk. Recently she visited our church here in St. Petersburg. As she stood before the congregation and unfurled the architects' drawing of her new school for Korean orphans, her eyes flashed and her face lit up. This humble Christian woman is devoting the entire proceeds of her books to this cause. She dares attempt great things for God.

Or think of young Dr. Mellon, scion of the fabulously wealthy Mellon family. As a young man, he wondered what to do with his life. Then one day he went to visit Dr. Albert Schweitzer at his hospital in Africa. That visit changed his life. He could never live small, think small, or plan small, after that. He prepared himself to serve as a missionary physician and is devoting the millions which otherwise might have been spent for pleasure on his hospital. Here the natives can come and avail themselves of Christian love and care. Persons of this kind literally scoop up the spirit of the crucified Lord into their lives, until it spills over into the lives of others. This is true greatness.

Peter and the other disciples got themselves so full of the light that shone in the face of Jesus that they could not help but reflect it. We must stand in the sunlight or we will not cast the shadow. It is when we turn to the light that the healing shadow falls behind us.

When Holman Hunt announced that he was going to

paint a picture of Jesus, his friends laughed at him. "You can only paint what you see," they said. "Anything else would be visionary." Holman Hunt replied, "But I will *see* Him. I will stand by His side when He works in the carpenter shop in Nazareth. I will accompany Him when He goes out to the multitude to heal the sick. I will watch Him as He performs the mighty miracle of raising the dead to life. I will follow Him to Calvary and look up and acknowledge that He died for me, and for the world. I will stand beside Mary Magdalene as she ecstatically calls Him 'Lord' at His resurrection."

As you stand and look at Holman Hunt's famous painting, *The Light of the World*, you readily acknowledge that he *saw* Jesus.

So may it be for all of us! God so fill us with His Light, that we cannot help but cast our healing shadow!

4 THE LIBERATING SECRET

"... God, who had set me apart from birth and called me through His grace, chose to reveal His Son to me and through me ...."

(Galatians 1:15, 16, NEB)

ARE YOU ONE of the many persons who are living a defeatist, negative life in these difficult days? Are you trying to make life's sums add up right, but without success? If so, here are two incidents — one out of contemporary life, and the other out of the pages of the New Testament — which will hearten and encourage you.

Recently I had a very interesting letter from a minister serving a large church in a northern city. He told me how for many years he had played the big game of pretense, pushing a narrow margin of strength to the limit, only to find himself spiritually and mentally exhausted. Then, at wit's end, casting his frail self upon a strength and a grace not his own, he found grace to help in time of need, and a secret — indeed a liberating secret. His human extremity became God's opportunity.

The other incident shines like a beacon through a third of our New Testament. You will find it glowing through all those beautiful epistles of St. Paul. This poor, pushing, straining, wretched man named Saul encounters the living

37

Christ on Damascus Road. From then on life was different. It wasn't the same life at all, in fact. You say you have read the story in the ninth chapter of the Acts of the Apostles. That you know about it. But has its significance really dawned on you? Has it "happened" to you?

In the first chapter of the letter to the Galatians, the great epistle of the Spirit, Paul shares the secret of his new found life. "God," he says, "who had set me apart from birth and called me through His grace, chose to reveal His Son to me and through me, in order that I might proclaim him among the gentiles" (Galatians 1:15, 16, New English Bible). This was the man who, next to Christ Himself, lived the greatest life ever lived on this earth.

Possibly you have run across the book entitled, *The Liberating Secret* by Norman Grubb, a radiant British Christian. Isn't it thrilling to think that the same experience which was Paul's could also be that of Norman Grubb, Hudson Taylor, John Wesley, and may also be our own? Remember, too, that many of these radiant Christians also had their spiritual struggles and had to be lifted out of darkness into light, out of defeat into victory.

We are frustrated because we feel ourselves cut off from very life itself. We, too, must have our Damascus Road experience. God must reveal His Son in us. Only in this way can we know the liberating secret. We will no longer ask God to patch up these old, frustrated, broken, sinful lives of ours. In fact, God doesn't operate on that basis at all. What God is waiting to do is to release *the life of His Son in us,* until there is an invisible union between ourselves and Jesus Christ. Christ Himself living out His life in us — *this* is the liberating secret. Christ living His own life in and through Paul — that was the victory. This is what the saints called the secret of "exchanged strength." This also marks the end of false burdens and false worries. We stop thinking our own selfish thoughts and have the

mind of Christ. In fact, everything our Heavenly Father
has in store for us may be ours through faith. Victory comes
through the indwelling Christ of the Holy Spirit. This indeed *is* a liberating secret!

Frances Ridley Havergal, the famous hymn writer,
tells us what this secret meant to her:

> Jesus, Thy life is mine,
> Dwell evermore in me.
> And let me see,
> That nothing can untwine
> Thy life from mine.
> Thy life in me be shown,
> Lord, I would henceforth seek
> To think and speak
> Thy thoughts, Thy words alone —
> No more my own.

Like all great things, there is mystery and marvel in this!
We can't explain it, but we can experimentally know the
glory and the power of it. If and when it happens to us,
there will be some rather revolutionary results in our lives.

For one thing, we will be more concerned with our
character than about our reputation. Reputation has to do
with what others think they know about you, whereas
character is what you and God know to be true about yourself. What a great relief to be through with pretense and
just to be what we were meant to be! Modern man seems
so concerned about the "image" the public holds of him,
which can be something entirely different than his true self.
But character is not this! Christian character is letting Jesus
Christ be reflected through your life. It is your life, with
its shortcomings and limitations, utterly yielded to the
sway of Another, until His divine Lordship is supreme over
all of life. The great Socrates once prayed the prayer,
"O God, I pray that the outer and the inner man may be
one." Reputation may be a bubble and a fiction. Solid

Christian character, after the example of Jesus Christ, is something far different.

Years ago while attending college, I secured a part-time job with a band instrument concern in a midwestern city. We had a large repair department to which people brought all manner of broken things. But we also had beautiful new instruments on display in our store counters. People would come by and look at them by the hour. Somehow, I always felt sorry for the people who brought in an old, battered instrument for repair! When the instrument was sent down from the repair room, it looked good, to be sure, and yet it was still the same old instrument, patched up. The tone left much to be desired. On the other hand, what a joy it was to sell to a purchaser an entirely new instrument, fresh from the hands of the maker! What wonderful music it made! There is nothing like the *original* when it comes to the true, Christian life.

A morally discouraged and defeated man once wondered what he should do with his life. He had come close to the brink. Then the thought came to him that it was God, the Heavenly Father, who had created him, and that the sensible thing was to go to his Maker and ask for help. "He understands me, and can help me, because He made me," said this man. How right he was!

The liberating secret? What is it? It is letting Christ, the Redeemer and Saviour of men, live out His own glorious life in and through you. It is reopening the enterprise of your life under new management. That way lies victory.

Let us go a step farther. When you know the secret of exchanged strength you stop hoarding your life, hanging on to your flagging, diminishing resources, saving yourself. You are no longer a limited reservoir but a dynamic, open channel through which Christ sends his limitless stores of love and power. It has been said that even a straw, lying prostrate on the water, can feel the tides of the ocean flowing through it. You experience the principle of released power — God's power and love revealed *through* you. Here for instance is Paul saying, "It pleased God, the Omnipotent, to release His power through me." This, of course, is life in the dimension of the Holy Spirit.

The charismatic revival of our time makes much of the baptism of the Holy Spirit. This emphasis is nothing new. It is simply the power of the Living Christ taking up His abode in our hearts and living out His life in us. We live in a new dimension. We cease being strangers to God's covenant of grace. To use a phrase of Dr. Elton Trueblood, we are no longer "cut-flower Christians."

In 1949, twelve top-ranking communists were on trial before Judge Harold Medina in the United States District Court, in the Southern District of New York. They tried to humiliate and aggravate Judge Medina, to make him lose his nerve. However, this plot of the communists did not come off, for Judge Medina is not only a great jurist but a believing Christian. He took time enough to meditate and to pray about the matter. He felt within himself the principle of released power — a power these communists knew nothing about. Let Judge Medina himself tell of his experience.

> If ever a man felt the presence of Someone standing beside him strengthening his will and giving him aid and comfort, I certainly did on that day. After all is said and done, it is not we who pull the strings; we are not the masters, but the servants of the Master's will, and it is well we should know it to be so.[1]

Andrew Murray, great man of prayer, used to say, "We have a God who delights in impossibilities!"

[1] Amos Lundquist, *Lives That Glorify God* (Philadelphia: Fortress Press, 1953), p. 47.

Not only does the liberating secret make us more concerned about our characters than our reputation and assure us of an inward "exchanged strength," but it enables God to unfold His plan for our lives. We tear up our selfish little blueprints and let Christ "take over." We no longer fear the future, for that is already in the hands of God. Like those Chinese Christians during war time, we too will write over our lives, "We do not know what is coming, but we know *who* is coming." This gives us a built-in serene confidence. We are "in the groove" — the groove of abiding trust in God and saving faith in Christ. We share in the eternal purpose which God purposed in Christ Jesus (Ephesians 3:11).

After telling us how God revealed His Son in and through him, Paul tells us what happened. People were led to say in amazement that the man who had persecuted them now preached the faith he had once tried to destroy. And they glorified God for what had happened.

When our travel party drove through rural England and Scotland, we were much interested in the quaint little cottages with thatched roofs. We found out that a great deal of skill goes into the making of these roofs and that they are thoroughly storm proof. The experience of entering one of these cottages and visiting with those who lived there reminded me of a story I read years ago. It concerned an old Scottish Elder. As he lay dying, his devoted and only daughter came to him and said, "Father, would you like me to ask the minister to come and read to you from the Book and say a prayer?" To which she received the forthright reply, "No, no, it is too late for that now. I thatched ma hoose in the calm weather."

Recall the words of Jesus in the parable in which He said that when a house is founded on the rock, the winds of adversity and trial can beat upon it, but it will stand fast!

That is the way to build a life. And that kind of life knows the liberating secret as we have been describing it in this chapter.

Do you know this liberating secret? Is the living Christ, by the Holy Spirit, living out His life in you? If so, you will be able to say with Frances Havergal:

> Jesus, my life is Thine,
> And evermore shall be
> Hidden in Thee!
> For nothing can untwine
> Thy life from mine.

Absolutely nothing!

5 A BEAUTY CONTEST WORTH WINNING

(*Proverbs* 31:25-29)

LONG YEARS AGO there was a beauty contest in Israel. No worldly prizes were given out. No pictures appeared in newspapers. But the winner revealed a beauty of soul that haunts our hearts across the ages. This woman was not a siren to lead weak men astray, but a saint who inspired them heavenward.

Here are a few of the winning qualities the judges wrote down, as recorded in the 31st chapter of the Book of Proverbs: strength, dignity, modesty, wisdom, loyalty, reverence for God. What a galaxy of sacred values these are!

A make-up expert recently stated that to prepare an actress to appear on the stage takes from thirty to forty minutes of careful work. According to his conception, beauty is from without. It is something that can be mechanically put on. Women in our day are being urged to make themselves physically attractive — good counsel, as far as it goes.

But some of us do not hold this idea of beauty at all. Quite the contrary, we believe that real beauty is from within. John Ruskin, an expert in the field of art, once said that our faces and bodies take on the hue and color of the thoughts we constantly entertain. Actually, we are the sculptors of our own characters, and these characters are

44

reflected in our faces. Abraham Lincoln stated that a man is responsible for the character of his face, even after his middle years.

In the 31st chapter of Proverbs we have a catalog of the qualities that won out in this beauty contest in Israel. These sovereign spiritual qualities never change. As the criteria of evaluating true beauty they abide.

Suppose, then, that we look over the shoulders of the judges and see what they consider to be the kind of beauty contest worth winning. What are some of the qualifications we find written down?

After stating that a virtuous woman is far above the price of rubies, we find stated the first hallmark of real beauty: "Strength and dignity are her clothing" (Proverbs 31:25, RSV). In other words, she wore these qualities like the apparel of a queen. This woman had an integrity of character that commended her to her fellowmen. She appealed to what was highest and noblest in them.

Evangeline Booth of Salvation Army fame was a woman of striking beauty as well as character. For many years she labored in the slums of east London, seeking to lead men to Christ. It was said of her that an invisible halo seemed to protect her wherever she went. Day or night she was never molested. I personally believe that men, however fallen and depraved, still respect this sovereign note of character in a woman. If the women of our day wish to be respected by men, then they must stand higher than the dull average! The New Testament teaching is that we are to present our bodies and spirits a living sacrifice unto the Lord, and to keep ourselves unspotted from the world. The most ghastly sight this side of perdition is a woman from whom the divine qualities of character have departed. "She that liveth in pleasure is dead while she liveth" (I Timothy 5:6).

Marlene Dietrich, who is something of an authority on beauty, was once quoted as saying that if a fraction of the analysis, attention and care given daily to outward beauty were given to inward beauty, the lot of mankind would be greatly improved. The wise Socrates once said, "I pray Thee, O God, that I may be beautiful within."

> What is beauty? Not the show
> Of shapely limbs and features. No.
>   These are but flowers
>   That have their dated hours,
> To breathe their momentary sweets, then go.
>   'Tis the stainless soul within
>   That outshines the fairest skin.
>   —*Sir A. Hunt*

Some clergymen gathered together, on one occasion, to discuss the various versions of the Bible. A number of opinions were given. One of these men listened to what the others had to say about their favorite version or translation, and then quietly remarked that he liked his mother's version of the Bible the best. His mother not only read the Bible, he said, but lived it out in love and deed.

Here now is another of the criteria the judges wrote down: "She opens her mouth with wisdom, and the teaching of kindness is on her tongue. She looks well to the ways of her household, and does not eat the bread of idleness" (Proverbs 31:26, 27, RSV). No wonder her husband praised her and her children rose up to call her blessed! What a wise strategist, this woman! She put first things first in her life. She knew where to make her influence felt for lasting good.

There is a story about the late Principal Rainey. For a time he was the center of a stormy theological controversy. A friend asked him on one occasion how he could keep serene and calm in the midst of all the abuse heaped on him.

We are told that Rainey quietly replied: "I am very happy at home."

God bless the noble army of women, both married and single, who have contributed so much to our welfare in careers outside the home. We think of women who have served well in the field of politics and statesmanship, in the profession of teaching, in our hospitals as nurses and doctors, and in the business world. What a blank page there would be in the progress of humanity without women like Frances Willard, Florence Nightingale and Madame Curie. And yet, strange creatures that we are, if you will ask the average man what the term womanhood brings to his mind, he will utter such words as these: mother, wife, companion, children, home. Recall the old Chinese proverb which states that while it takes 100 men to make an encampment, it takes a woman to make a home.

If you were sometime to visit our Churchmen's Club here in St. Petersburg, at their monthly meeting, you would hear the men singing some old-fashioned ditties. One of the favorites is the following:

> I want a girl, just like the girl
> That married dear old Dad.
> She was a pearl, and the only girl
> That Daddy ever had.
> A good old-fashioned girl with heart so true.
> One who loves nobody else but you.
> I want a girl, just like the girl
> That married dear old Dad.

What is more, the men not only sing these words, they mean them!

Next to the presence of God in a home is the dedicated presence of a Christian mother. We are short, desperately short, of this quality of Christian womanhood in the America of our day. Our disgraceful statistics on delinquency, both juvenile and adult, as well as our high divorce rate, are

eloquent testimony to this fact. Our human society is fall-
ing apart for the lack of a basic Christian integrity, primarily on the part of American womanhood.

During the time the Kinsey Report on the morals of
American men and women was being formulated, one of the
reporters found himself on an airplane making a transcon-
tinental flight. He was weary of soul, having seen so much
of the sordid side of human nature. He felt he had been
living in a pig-sty. Presently he noticed a young couple
not far from where he sat on the plane earnestly engaged in
conversation. They were already making plans for the future of the two- or three-year-old son with them. In fact,
they were thinking of another little one soon to be born
in their home. They spoke fondly of their home church
and community. Was it not John R. Mott who said, "If
God is your partner, you can afford to make big plans"?
So with this young couple. The reporter got off the plane
a different man. He felt as though he had taken a clean
shower; all the dirt and grime that had accumulated were
washed from him. This was real living.

Now let us take a last glance at these qualities which
won a beauty contest so long ago. Look again over the
judge's shoulders and you will read the words, "Charm is
deceitful, and beauty is vain, but a woman who fears the
Lord is to be praised" (Proverbs 31:30, RSV). Here, in
one deft stroke of the pen, is the consummate virtue of all.
This woman is first of all a God-fearing woman. In His
constant presence her children are taught the difference
between right and wrong, the meaning of holiness, and
the lessons of obedience, honesty, kindness and reverence.

John Wesley tells us in his *Journal* of the passing of his
remarkable mother, Susannah Wesley. Let him speak for
himself:

About three in the afternoon I went to my mother and found her change was near. . . . Her look was calm and serene, and her eyes focused upward, while we commended her soul to God. From three to four, the silver cord was loosing, and the wheel breaking on the cistern; and then, without any struggle, or sigh, or groan, the soul was set at liberty. We stood round the bed and fulfilled her last request, uttered a little before she lost her speech: "Children, as soon as I am released, sing a psalm of praise to God" (entry for August 23, 1742).

The word that best describes this kind of mother is the word *godly*. Truly, she fears the Lord.

One has the feeling, too, that this woman of yesteryear was a woman of the Word. In his *Fors Clavigera*, John Ruskin testifies to his mother's knowledge of the Bible. It was the 119th Psalm which she early inculcated in the character of her boy, and which all through his life remained with him. He was taught that the law of the Lord was perfect, converting the soul. Before he was thirteen years old, she had taken him six times through the Bible. In another of his writings, the "Praeterita," he tells us that this maternal installation of his mind was what stayed with him longest, and was most effective in the building of his character. It was more important than all other book learning.

Then also you have the feeling that this mother, because she was God-fearing and Bible-loving, was a woman of prayer. She bound that family of hers with golden chains about the feet of God.

A newspaper reporter called me recently to ask assistance in an article she proposed to write on how to acquaint children with the fact of death. What can one possibly say to a small child on such a subject? She told me she would spend several days in the library, looking up all sorts of things, seeking to get a stance for the writing of this difficult article.

I suggested that she open the New Testament and there she would find a knowledge far more effective and penetrating than she could find in any other book. In its pages she would find the words of the Lord Jesus Christ, who is the Way, the Truth and the Life, and who loved little children as none other ever did. I suggested that if children were faithfully taught the meaning of the Christian faith, they would not fear death. That if they were acquainted with Christ who is and gives life eternal, they would be possessed of an assurance that would strip fear from the face of death. That to know God aright — the God who revealed himself in Jesus Christ — is to have, already in this life, life eternal. "I am the resurrection and the life" said the Lord. "He who believes in me, though he die, yet shall he live, and whoever lives and believes in me shall never die" (John 11:25, 26, rsv). Teach children these words of Jesus Christ and they will never fear death.

God give us in the America of our day mothers who are possessed of this strong Christian faith. The time will come when their children will rise up and call them blessed. And the most fitting epitaph that can be written in their honor, will be the glorious words of the 31st chapter of Proverbs: "Charm is deceitful, and beauty is vain, but a woman who fears the Lord is to be praised. Give her of the fruit of her hands, and let her works praise her in the gates"!

6 WHAT WE CAN LEARN FROM THE ENEMY

"For the children of this world are in their generation wiser than the children of light." (*Luke* 16:8)

WHILE GOING THROUGH Boston Common several years ago,
a friend and I noticed a large group of people gathered
about an impassioned young orator. We did not have to
listen long to become aware of his message. He was preaching the gospel, not according to Jesus Christ, but according to Karl Marx, Lenin and Stalin. He was urging on his
listeners the familiar tenets of communism: class war, the
dictatorship of the proletariat, dialectical materialism, the
godless society. As we went on our way, my friend remarked
that if only we could muster the enthusiasm of this young
communist behind our Christian message, the Kingdom
of God would come. We would move heaven and earth
for the Christian cause.

Jesus spoke a word to His disciples over 1900 years ago
which we need to take to heart today: "the children of this
world are wiser in their generation than the children of
light" (Luke 16:8). In his translation, Dr. Moffatt brings out
the full meaning of these words: "the children of this
world *look further ahead* in dealing with their own generation, than the children of Light." You see what this means.
The so-called "children of this world" — the communists,

51

the secularists, the unbelievers, and their kind — are shrewd, cunning and ruthless. Sometimes they outwit us followers of Christ. St. Paul refers to them in Philippians 3:18, as the "enemies of the cross of Christ."

Men like J. Edgar Hoover of our Federal Bureau of Investigation, Allen Dulles, former head of our Central Intelligence Bureau, Max Eastman and Eugene Lyons, who write with a deep insight concerning current events, are not alarmists. However, they point to the handwriting on the wall, and warn us that ours is a day of decision. The great question of our time can be put quite simply: Will we — can we — muster sufficient spiritual morale to parry the thrust of militant communism and godlessness? This question has to do with our ultimate loyalties. Our free world, so-called, must undergo a profound spiritual reawakening in order to endure.

What then did our Lord mean when He said that the children of this world outwit us? In what way are they wiser? Is there something that we can learn from the enemy? Suppose we try and answer that question realistically and honestly.

To begin with, the enemy of the Cross holds his faith with a deadly seriousness that often shames us nominal Christians. He is not casual as so many of us are. Rarely is he guilty of uttering that inanity, "It doesn't matter what a man believes so long as he lives a good, moral life." The creed of dialectical materialism, with its complete blackout of God and spiritual values, may appear to be nonsense to us, but it is dangerous nonsense! Already there are forty million communists inhabiting one-fourth of the world's territory, and one-third of the world's three billion people.[1]

The Third World War, as someone has called it, moves

[1] From report given by J. Edgar Hoover, Appropriations Sub-Committee of the House of Representatives, 1964.

on the ideological front. The battle that is on in the world today is for the human mind. It has to do with *ideas.*

Listen, for instance, to that cocky communist, Mr. Khrushchev, when he says: "We can win this war without firing a shot. Victory for our side is inevitable." Communism, he insists, resides in the logic of things. It is imbedded in the processes of history. Hence, the enemy makes me more appreciative and grateful for my own divinely revealed Christian faith with its teaching about God, the soul, the redemption that is in Christ Jesus, the Kingdom of God. I believe that God and truth are on the side of this Christian faith of ours, and that what we need to do is to lay hold on it with a new seriousness of purpose. And at this point, as I have indicated, communism can teach us something.

In his book, *This Is My Story,* Louis Francis Buddenz, now an avowed Christian, wonders at the zeal with which he once held the teachings of communism. He refers to it as "the mesmerism of unbelief." Once, he says, Marxism had provided him with a philosophy of life. Here was something to be believed, something to live and die for. He did not realize the terrible falsity of this creed until he finally turned from it to the Christian faith.

George McLeod of the Iona Community in Scotland, tells how a youthful recruit to Marxism once confided to him, "You Christians have actually got the message the world needs, if you only knew how to get it across."

The enemy also has a Master Plan and Time Table for world conquest. At a time when the average Christian is contributing $1.75 a year for world evangelism, the communist thinks and plans *big.* He marches toward his goals with banners flying and bugles blowing. He is militant about putting his "religion" to work. He claims the world for his pagan gods.

The two main weapons of communism are those of in-

filtration and subversion. These constitute what Max Eastman refers to as the "tactic of the gradual challenge." In
this respect, the enemy has something to teach us. Communism seldom makes a frontal attack. Rather is it a case
of "here a little and there a little." We might say that
communism insinuates itself into the processes and events of
our day.

Thus the enemy seeks to infiltrate the mind of youth.
He uses the tactic of the Big Lie. When I was in Europe
a few years ago, I saw communism at work in East Germany.
Here was communist youth in its green garb, marching and
chanting its slogans on the streets of the East German sec-
tor. Communism has already brought over 700,000 German youth under its sway in East Germany alone. It has
profaned the Christian rite of Confirmation and is giving
to youth its own secular version which, of course, leaves
God out entirely. Eighty-eight per cent of East German
youth is under the control of the godless society. Everywhere you look in East Germany you can see communism
shrieking its slogans from the walls of the buildings round
about.

Likewise, communism wants to worm its way into our
institutions of learning. It succeeds wherever there is a
spiritual vacuum, and where the Biblical, spiritual aims of
education are lost sight of.

It seeks to subvert toward its own ends the restless
discontent to be found in the ranks of labor, and our racial
groupings.

It seeks to subvert the legitimate aspirations of the
rising peoples of the world for nationhood. We have only
to look at Cuba, the Congo, and Southeast Asia to see
present evidence of this fact.

Yes, communism "wants in" on our religion and church
life, too! It finds its opportunity wherever the great bastions of the Christian faith are discarded or held lightly.

Let me give you an illustration. In one of our southern newspapers not long ago, an ad appeared which, on the surface of it, looked very harmless. It urged people to be free from the so-called trammels and teachings of evangelical Christianity. It promised them a free mind" and an intelligent faith if they forsook their evangelical, Biblical faith. We do not want a coercive type of religion in our churches — so ran this ad.

Now, let me say that I glory as much in the "free mind" as do others. But let us not be taken in by the specious promise that we shall become "free" by tearing up the divine blueprint of our faith. If that day ever comes, we shall have nothing with which to resist the godless tide.

This is the time for us to remember that Christianity has its own timetable and blueprint for world conquest. Jesus brought it with Him when he returned in the power of the Spirit to His home town of Nazareth. While at the synagogue in Nazareth, He stood up to read from the great prophecy of Isaiah, chapter 61. What wonderful words these are:

> The Spirit of the Lord is upon me, because he hath anointed me to preach the gospel to the poor; he hath sent me to heal the brokenhearted, to preach deliverance to the captives, and recovering of sight to the blind, to set at liberty them that are bruised, to preach the acceptable year of the Lord.

Then He looked around upon His amazed fellow townsmen and said, "This day is this scripture fulfilled in your ears."

What a marvelous faith to put to work in this day of need! What a time for us to win the mind of youth for Christ and His Cause; to reach out a hand of Christian altruism to the rising nations of the earth; to set a Christian example in our own racial and social relationships; in a word, to abolish the breeding places of communism wherever we may find them. In our day we need the revolutionary faith of men like John R. Mott, Sherwood Eddy, and others who said, "The world for Christ in our generation." We need to hear again our Lord when He said, "The Kingdom of God is at hand. Repent ye and believe the gospel!"

There is a story about a Washington, D.C., cabbie who was driving some foreign visitors around the capital city. When he was asked what the words, "What is past is prologue," on the Archives Building meant, he replied, "I'll tell you what they mean; they mean, 'You ain't seen nothing yet!'"

Christianity in our day needs to become again a crusading faith. In this respect, the children of this world look further ahead in dealing with their generation than do the children of light, as our Lord indicated. We need to regain the initial zeal of the Christians of the first century.

If there is one other thing the enemy can teach us, it is that the Cause has precedence over the individual. Here, for instance, are words from Lenin: "It is not your spare time that I want, but your whole lives." Recall Hitler's statement, "It's your *souls* we want." He then proceeded to lead a whole generation of German youth astray.

But let us not forget that our Master, Jesus Christ said that we are to put the Kingdom *first* in our lives. Think, for instance, of these unforgettable words of His: "He that is willing to lose his life for my sake and the gospel's, shall find it." Here you have two types of totalitarianism: one pagan, and the other divine. We must get our priorities right!

We must become aware again that freedom is not free. It costs. And the day of the martyrs is not yet done. Thousands of Christians in the world of our day are laying down their lives for Christ and His Kingdom.

Nor is freedom inevitable. Goethe was right when he said that freedom must be won anew in every generation. Christian freedom, as we have it in Christ, is not a part-time undertaking. It is a full-time job.

This means that all of us, school teachers, businessmen, parents, professional men, youth, must dedicate ourselves with a new devotion to our blessed heritage! Early Christianity won in the Roman arena because those first Christians could say like Paul, "For me to live is Christ; to die is gain." They were men and women of whom the world was not worthy. They were Christ's minutemen. They outlived, out-thought and out-died their pagan contemporaries. They still do.

A few years ago in Boston, Massachusetts, the pageantry of Paul Revere's midnight ride was reenacted. A lantern was hung up in the tower of Old North Church, and at midnight a man rode horseback all the way from Boston to Lexington Green. It was very picturesque, to be sure. We do well to ask ourselves, however: granted that we have the pageantry, do we also have the conviction that once went with it? In the memorable words of Lowell's poem, "The Present Crisis":

> Some great cause, God's new Messiah,
> Offering each the bloom or blight —
> Parts the goats upon the left hand,
> And the sheep upon the right.

What side are we on?

A friend recently handed me a letter he received from a Finnish boy who was on the battle front at the time communism was invading Finland. Here are a few lines from that letter:

> My brother Nicolai and I are in the reserves under our country's orders, our country of which we love every stump as if it were a part of us, and for which we are willing to give our humble lives if so cruel a fate

is to be ours. We have inherited from our forefathers
the will to defend our nation. They had to leave their
plows standing idle — while together they took up arms
against those who threatened to rob them of their liveli-
hood. So we follow in the path of our forefathers!
That desire burns in the heart of every man and woman
of us. War we do not love. But when we are threatened
by seizure of values we simply cannot surrender, then
we will not yield as long as there is a single one of us
left standing. We'll last till we die at our defense line!

Our Christian heritage is either worth *that*, or nothing!

7 THE CHRISTIAN LORD'S DAY

"The sabbath was made for man, and not man for
the sabbath."   (*Mark* 2:27)

DURING THE DAYS of the Second World War, an American
serviceman wrote a letter to his loved ones at home. In
this letter he told them how he managed to keep the spirit
of the Christian Sabbath. Here was a boy, thousands of
miles from home, quite likely lonely and a bit distraught,
yet true to his basic convictions. He told his loved ones
how he tried to synchronize his own personal observance
of Sunday with theirs. "When I think you are in church,"
he said, "where I myself would love so much to be, I just
open my Bible, read a few verses and, in the inner temple
of my heart, say a prayer for you and the welfare of all
men."

That is pretty good, isn't it, for a lad thousands of miles
from home, seeking to keep the spirit of the Sabbath
inviolate? The remembrance of that Christian Sabbath
in his home held him fast and strong and true. Someone
has truly said that Sunday is the core of our civilization —
a day dedicated to thought and reverence.

Now let us make it clear that we are not advocating
blue-lawism. Not at all. We are not pleading in this chap-

ter for a revival of the kind of Sabbath our Lord had to contend with in His day, or even for a return of the Puritan Sabbath of early New England.

This is not to say that I do not greatly admire the spirit of those old-timers of the Puritan Commonwealth. We moderns can hardly afford to give "three sneers" for the Puritans! They might have been somewhat somber and forbidding, but believe me, they had something we need today. They had moral backbone.

I have been reading up on some of the quaint customs of the Puritan Sabbath. Imagine sermons three hours long! What in the world would some of you, who have trouble keeping awake twenty or thirty minutes, ever do on that basis! And some of their habits were quaint to say the least. Did you know, for instance, that they had a tithing man whose duty it was, whenever he saw someone's head nodding, to give them a strong rap on the head with a long pole? Personally, I am glad we have a better use for our deacons today! In Virginia they had a custom of passing around a snuff box when someone got sleepy. What a cure for boring sermons! Yet with it all, our admiration goes out to those stern souls who laid the keel for our nation.

Then there were the rather weird and strange customs of the Pharisees of Jesus' day. A woman was not allowed to look in a mirror, because if she did she might see a gray hair and try to pull it out, and that would be breaking the Sabbath! People were not allowed to wear artificial teeth on the Sabbath day. So, as someone has suggested, the saints did not look their prettiest on the Sabbath. And so on and on — *ad nauseam.*

But none of that for our Lord Jesus Christ! He rescued the ancient Sabbath from its negative misuse and translated it into a radiant, positive, glad day. So much so that today we have a hymn in which we sing: "O day of rest and gladness, most beautiful, most bright."

Jesus in fact transfigured the ancient Sabbath through His own victory over death — so that today we keep not the seventh day of the week, but the first, the Christian Lord's Day, as a memorial to His great victory over the "last enemy."

When His contemporaries criticized His hungry disciples for plucking a few ears of grain on the Sabbath, Jesus held them at bay. When they criticized Him for healing the sick, He replied, "The sabbath was made for man, and not man for the sabbath," and then added, "the Son of man is Lord also of the sabbath." He claimed dominion over this day, and because it is His day, it is ours also — His gift to us.

Jesus made it clear that the Christian Lord's Day is not a day for idle gossip, for sitting around with hands folded piously. Indeed not! It is a day for good deeds. A day to be kept in the spirit of reverence, service and worship.

Now we are concerned that this day is at stake in our modern world and society. We need to become aware of that fact. Dr. Leslie Weatherhead, eminent British clergyman at City Temple in London, said in one of his sermons that hardly ten per cent of the English people attend church regularly. Hear his own words: "Unless we take a moral stand for this day, our children will have no Sunday worth talking about."

What then, shall we do with regard to Sunday? Shall we surrender it, or shall we stand fast in the spirit of Christian witness for it? Are we willing to do battle for it?

Let me point out a few pertinent facts as they have to do with our Lord's Day.

Surely, the physical and spiritual well-being of man demands that one day in seven be devoted to other than secular pursuits. Our Lord recognized this when He said that the Sabbath was made for man. To Him, this was not a day of luxury but of necessity.

Oliver Wendell Holmes once said, "He who ordained the Sabbath loved the poor." In other words, this day was not gotten up by religious fanatics and die-hards, but was created by the finger of God. The infinite and eternal Creator knew the need of His creatures for this day.

There is a spiritual rhythm about life, and we get into trouble when we desert it. Ask the doctors and nurses, as well as the ministers and psychiatrists who deal with people. They will tell you that one out of every ten hospital beds throughout America is occupied by the mentally ill. If the Christian Sabbath was needed in the life of yesterday, it is far more needed in our day, with its high pace of living. Or ask Christian businessmen, of which there are not a few here in America. They are willing to stand up and witness for the need of this day. One of them said to me recently, "Anyone ought to be able to see the common-sense value of keeping one day in seven for rest, recreation and worship." He added that if we lose our nerve and let this day go into limbo, then legislation would be needed to help keep us mentally sane and balanced.

Certainly those who toil and work in the heat of the day on our modern assembly lines need the Christian Lord's Day. There is a spiritual and mental rhythm in life which we desert to our peril. We need to keep the Christian Sabbath holy.

Once, while he was addressing the Lancashire Miners, the great Britisher John Bright quoted the words of George Herbert:

> Without thy light, the week were dark,
> Thy torch doth show the way.

He was speaking of the need and place of the Christian Sabbath.

Not only do we need to observe one day in seven for the physical and spiritual well-being of humans, but let us recognize that those who would scuttle the Christian Sabbath are not our friends, much as they may pretend to be. Nor are they working for the best interests of the American community.

Many years ago a group of worldly minded men founded a community far out on the west coast of this nation. There was one stipulation, namely, that there would be no Sunday observance. No Christian Church. No Christian minister. Well, they got it, and lived to regret it! What happened in this wide open town? Law observance went by the board. You do not have law-abiding people, apart from the influence of the Church. Property values went down. People could not get credit in the business world. No one much wanted to move there. The youth of the community got into trouble. Home life languished. The ordinary decencies that make life bearable went by the board. These hard-headed men eventually admitted their mistake. They said, "It is clear that we cannot found a civilized community apart from a Christian church. We're going to send for the best preacher we can get." And they did.

In his book *Foundations for Reconstruction,* Dr. Elton Trueblood tells of the importance of the Sabbath in ancient Judah, especially while Judah was in captivity in Babylon starting in the year 586 B.C. Here was a religious people in an utterly pagan environment. The northern kingdom, Israel, had fallen more than 100 years before and had never revived. Only one thing saved the southern kingdom and that was the institution of the Sabbath. Once

each week the people stood up as families to be counted
for God. Along with the Sabbath came the institution of the
synagogue where people heard the Word of God read,
and were reminded of their primal loyalties. A precious
heritage was saved from extinction by the observance of the
Sabbath.

Dr. Trueblood writes that many Americans today are
suffering from "the angelic fallacy." We think we do not
need the supports of institutional religion, that we can get
along on our own. The plain truth is that we are dependent
on the loyalties of the past, and that we are not angels, but
men with clay feet.

There are naturally some emergency services that have
to be carried on on Sunday. The faithful doctor must make
his call, the nurse must care for the sick, the Christian minister must give his sermon and lead his people. Our Lord
Jesus healed on the Sabbath and he claimed utter dominion over it. We are thinking rather of those secular
occupations which are gradually nosing their way into the
sacredness of the first day of the week.

You have heard the expression, have you not, "A camel's
nose in the tent"? It is the story of the Arab who fetched
up one night out on the desert, put up his tent, and having
staked his camel on the outside, lay down to sleep. He had
hardly gotten his first wink before the camel came and
nosed under the flap of the tent, looked around and thought,
"My! how nice it is in there." Then he went a little farther,
got his nose *and* his front legs in. Soon he got in his hump,
and his back legs, until in the last scene we find the Arab
on the outside of the tent, and the camel on the inside!
It was a complete "take over."

This camel of secularization has his nose definitely in
the American tent. He sells liquor to minors if he can
get by with it, and litters our newsstands with his porno-

graphic literature. He hawks and peddles his wares over our radio and television sets and in our newspapers. He cares not one whit for the moral and spiritual values which constitute the backbone of any civilized community. He wants to scuttle our Christian Lord's Day. He is out for a wide-open Sabbath.

You who are parents of small children already know how hard it is to keep a semblance of reverence on a Sunday. I think of that young mother who said to me, "First you battle the Sunday comics, fold the newspaper, and put it away. Then you turn the television off, and get the children scrubbed and dressed. Once in the car you almost break a speed law to get to church on time." Said she, "I made it, but I am almost done in!"

Either Christ is Lord of the Sabbath and the Sabbath is devoted to Christian ends, or we face the prospect of a godless and lawless nation and society. Only eternal vigilance can preserve what remains of our Lord's Day.

Let us also bear in mind that in this crucial hour of history, with thousands of her sons battling the evil of communism abroad, America needs her Lord's Day more than ever before.

The late Senator Toby of New Hampshire wrote a book which he entitled *The Return to Morals*. In it he emphasized the need for a return to morals in government and in the world at large. But how are we going to make such a "return" apart from a faithful observance of Sunday? The two main enemies we face in our day are communism and secularism. Both leave out everything sacred in our heritage: God, worship, the sacredness of personality, the Bible. If you want to know how secularism operates, just look around you. Surely you must be aware of the constant pressure of selfish interests seeking to break down your moral resistance. Many people have become neutral and noncommital in their attitudes. Basic spiritual values gradually dim out.

Do we need to be reminded at this point how communism works? This evil has taken over area after area of our modern world. On one occasion I talked with a Christian missionary who had been driven out of precommunist China. The communists did not abruptly go and padlock the door of his church. Instead, they called up on Saturday night and informed the missionary that his church building would be needed for other purposes at eleven o'clock Sunday morning. Lenin was right when he said that Christianity and the dialectic of communism cannot live side by side. Godlessness and Christianity have nothing in common. Believe me, my friends, the Christian Sabbath is not a Victorian relic out of the past, to be put in some museum. It is the gift of God to men — one of the few remaining bulwarks standing between civilization on one hand, and barbarism on the other. Truly, Sunday is the core of our civilization!

Here is one incident out of the past which can inspire us to be more militant and loyal when it comes to the preservation of our sacred day. An elderly man once related this experience to Dr. DeWitt Talmadge. He was one of a group rolling across the American prairie toward the gold coast. On Saturday night the covered wagon in which he and his companions were traveling halted at an outpost of civilization. The next day being Sunday, he was invited by the group to spend the day gambling. "I cannot do that," said this man, "for this is the Sabbath." The others laughed at him and said, "What do you mean, the Sabbath? There is no Sunday out here in the wilderness." "Oh, yes, there is," came the reply. "I brought it with me in my heart across the mountains." And so while the others gambled the day away, he took out his Bible and read, and like the American serviceman, with whom we began this chapter, he worshiped in that temple not made with hands.

I brought it with me across the mountains!

We began with a question, "Shall we surrender the Christian Lord's Day?" Let us now reply, "We shall not surrender this day. In the name of Him who is Lord of the Sabbath, our answer is 'No surrender!'"

8 CAN RELIGION MAKE ME WELL?

"And he could there do no mighty works, save that he laid his hands upon a few sick folk, and healed them."   (*Mark* 6:5)

A FEW YEARS ago an article entitled "Master, Heal Me" appeared in one of our popular magazines. It was the story of a man named Bob Stout, who had been seriously injured in a train accident. He had been given up by the physicians, but his wife never lost hope. She had implicit trust that God would restore her husband. And so with Bob's pastor and a prayer group in the church the Stouts attended, they prayed for this man's healing. God heard and answered their prayer, and Bob was miraculously healed.

When the story of this healing was reported abroad, there was skepticism in some quarters. This, of course, was to be expected. The Bible teaches that the natural — that is the unspiritual — man just doesn't understand the things of God. The fact is, some of the clergy even found fault with the methods that Bob's pastor had employed. Perhaps these good Christian people were just fooling themselves, and maybe the recovery of their friend was just a stroke of sheer luck!

There is a hard, brittle skepticism in the hearts of people in our day, and we who claim to be followers of Jesus must constantly be on guard. After all, why should not even good Christian people doubt the ability of God to heal, when we of the regular orthodox churches have surrendered the ministry of healing to the sects and the cults?

We read in the gospel of Mark that on one occasion, Jesus returned to His home town of Nazareth in the power of the Spirit. He was prepared to do great things for God there. The home folks, however, cold-shouldered Him. It was as though they said, "Who does he think he is, anyway? We know all about him! He had a carpenter shop down one of our side streets before he got fool notions into his head. And what is more, his mother and sisters and brothers are members of our synagogue!"

Did not Jesus Himself say that a prophet is without honor among his own kin-folk? The net result of His visit to Nazareth was that He could do no mighty works there. He managed, somehow, to lay His hands on a few sick people and heal them. But "no mighty works." Then this added touch: "And he marveled because of their unbelief!"

To Jesus, not skepticism but faith is the normal, healthy attitude in life. He was chagrined and disappointed at the tragic lack of life-giving faith of these people among whom He was raised.

In view of all the confusion there is on this subject, what can we believe about spiritual healing? Do you, for instance, believe that your religion can make you well, or better yet, keep you well? What is the relation, if any, between the mystery of the human mind and body? Has Jesus Christ still the power to release the spirit of abundant life and healing in these minds and bodies of ours which so tragically need it?

Suppose we think together about that in this chapter. Let me stress a few convictions which I believe to be pertinent and which I hope will be helpful.

Let us begin by stating that there can be no reasonable doubt that healing is an integral part of the Christian Gospel. It looks out at us from the joyous pages of the New Testament. You just cannot delete it and retain the good news of Jesus Christ. Here are two rather obvious facts: Jesus Christ Himself healed the sick, and He gave to His disciples power over disease.

The Great Physician Himself had compassion on the multitude. As William Newton Clarke once said: "His healing miracles are the outgrowth of His compassion." We read that when Jesus spoke, the power of God was present to heal. On more than one occasion people brought the sick and the lame, the halt and the blind to Him from all directions. And we read that He laid His hands on every one of them and healed them. When John the Baptist sent his disciples to ask Jesus if He was the promised Messiah, Jesus did not indulge in long arguments. Instead, He allowed these emissaries to witness His mighty works of healing, and then told them to go and tell John the things they had seen. These mighty works were evidence of the Kingdom of God among men.

Dr. Raymond Calkins once told of hearing Dr. Richard C. Cabot of Harvard read a paper on psychotherapy. At the close of the paper, Dr. Cabot was asked by someone present if he believed in the possibility of spiritual healing in the case of organic disease like cancer. The famous research physician replied: "I have never heard of a case of cancer being cured in that way. But I would like to say that I have never yet found myself in the presence of any disease which I myself felt unable to cure, or which I have never heard of anyone else curing in that way, without saying to myself, 'If there were someone here who had one hundred times the personality that I have, that disease might be cured in that way.'"[1] This is to say, of course, that there is

---

[1] *Treasury of the Christian World*, edited by A. Gordon Nasby (New York: Harper and Row, 1953), p. 161.

a power available through faith and prayer, which cannot be released otherwise, and that this power can accomplish wonders which are humanly impossible. Dr. Calkins rightly adds that it was the magnitude of Jesus' person that healed others. It was the impact of that profound personality on other lives that worked miracles of cure.

And His power and strength and purity overflowed in the lives of the disciples He sent out to heal. They had no power apart from Him, nor do we. He told them to go out and heal the sick in His name. And they did.

But now we must qualify that first statement of ours somewhat: although Jesus did heal the sick, He did not make bodily healing the *center* of His ministry. At Nazareth He laid His hands on a few sick folk and healed them — that was all. But again and again in the gospel records we find Him imploring those whom He had healed not to make a big noise about it. Why? Because He knew Himself to be the Son of God who came primarily as the Great Physician of the *soul*. The body in time decomposes into its native elements. But the soul is destined for eternity. In fact, it seems that the bodily cures of Jesus flow from healing at a much deeper level — the level of the heart.

Christ Jesus came into the world to save sinners (I Timothy 1:15). He came that men might be spiritually reborn from Above. He was concerned that the prodigal who had lost his way might return again to the Father's house. Again and again His words ring out — "Thy sins be forgiven thee. Rise, take up thy bed and walk!"

Almost twenty centuries before we moderns made mention of psychosomatic medicine, the Great Physician knew that our physical being could not be healthy if our souls and minds were sick!

It was — and still is — the *sin* problem which was the great problem.

Dr. C. H. Dodd, who has studied the original gospel sources as have few scholars, says: "It appears that the authority of Jesus penetrated to the subconscious depths of personality, where so many mysterious disorders of mind and body have their source." Yes, our Lord Jesus Christ understood men fully, knew what was in men, and spoke to the inner springs of the soul. And the soul heard and responded. He gave men the desire to be well. He gave them the will to live.

When recently I asked a leading psychiatrist what he made of the statement in the Apostles' Creed, "I believe in the forgiveness of sins," I received an amazing reply. "Why, apart from the knowledge of *that,* none of my patients ever really get well. The forgiveness of sins is the basic therapy."

According to the Mayo Clinic, about seventy-five per cent of illnesses are emotionally induced. Dr. Alfred Adler insists that most of the ills of human personality are due to our stubborn resistance to the truth Jesus taught, that it is more blessed to give than to receive. We need to master the fine art of giving ourselves away.

"I have found out," said a physician to a man who consulted him, "what is the matter with you. You are allergic to yourself!"

Again, if we really wish to be well (and to remain well) we need to realize the tremendous power of suggestion, in both its negative and positive aspects. We can actually think and talk ourselves into invalidism. Our Lord goes to Nazareth to do mighty works for God. The lame and halt and blind stretch out arms of entreaty to Him and are helped. But only they! The rest stand about doubtingly! A leading American statesman recently said that there will be no depression in America, unless we talk ourselves into one.

Now, turn from the power of negative suggestion to its positive aspect. When we worship God in spirit and in truth, we dare to turn our faith loose! We affirm that Jesus

Christ is the same "yesterday, today and forever," and that He is present wherever His followers are gathered together in His Name.

Here in our church in St. Petersburg, we have large congregations gathered from all over the world during our long tourist season from autumn to Easter. Standing in the pulpit of such a church, one can almost feel "lame hands of faith" stretched out with entreaty. People are present with all kinds of needs, and when the Holy Spirit is released to do His mighty work, people are healed of fear, guilt, anxiety and depression of spirit. They are released from self, and made free to serve and witness. In our balcony one Sunday, there sat a visitor beside one of our staff members. Said he, "I worshiped in this church some years ago. Things have not gone well with me since I have been away. I said to myself, if I can just get inside that church again and worship, I will be well." And then this: "I feel better already."

There you have the exercise of simple, availing faith. What this person was saying was simply, that if he could but touch the hem of Christ's garment at a church service, he would be healed. It is not we who heal, but the Great Physician who releases the healing power of love through us. And what an inspiring, wonderful thing to be channels for His using!

There remains the mystery of the "unhealed." All of us know of sincere and earnest Christians who have prayed for bodily healing, but seemingly in vain. Not all were healed in Jesus' day. Let's be frank and honest about it. What then can be said?

I have purposely used the word "mystery" in speaking of the unhealed. As yet we know so very little. I believe that God uses dedicated physicians and nurses as part of

His great healing ministry. If the pain cannot be removed, then perhaps it can be made more bearable.

We know persons with ailing bodies but radiant spirits! Even on an invalid's couch, the

> Soul can split the sky in two,
> And let the face of God shine through!
> —*Edna St. Vincent Millay*

Such gallant souls make us hardier ones ashamed of our futile complainings! They witness for Christ with their very sufferings.

Thank God, then, for the healing of the Resurrection, when God has promised to give His faithful sufferers a spiritual and immortal body. "This corruptible must put on incorruption, and this mortal must put on immortality" (I Corinthians 15:53). The radiant Paul who wrote these words speaks of the physical body as an old "tent" that must some day come down, and the sooner the better. "For we know that if the mere tent, which is our earthly house, is taken down, we have in heaven a building from God, a house not made by human hands, but eternal" (II Corinthians 5:1, Weymouth). No wonder he could shout, "Thanks be to God who gives us the victory through our Lord Jesus Christ!"

Dr. Bruce Wright tells of hearing Fannie Crosby, the blind hymn writer, sing one of her hymns before a large audience in Carnegie Hall. It was the beloved hymn, "Some Day the Silver Cord Will Break." There was a heavenly radiance on her face as she sang,

> And I shall see Him face to face,
> And tell the story saved by grace.

But it was when she put special emphasis on the word "see" that a thrill went through the audience. You could never forget it. Fannie Crosby was thinking, was she not, of the healing of the Resurrection? Her blind eyes would be opened, and she would see her Saviour face to face.

So let us not complain, nor limit the power of the Great Physician. Let us be His channels of sunshine and healing to others in their sufferings. Let us look away from our weaknesses to Christ in His power and His strength. And let us pray as did those first disciples, astonished as they were in His presence — "Lord, increase our faith!"

9 WAS JESUS REALLY DIVINE?

"Thou art the Christ, the Son of the living God."
(*Matthew* 16:16)

A YOUNG SEMINARIAN was confiding his theological difficulties to a trusted friend. Said he, "I have difficulty in knowing how to think about Jesus. Somehow I cannot think of Him as being divine. I can only accept Him if He is an ordinary man like the rest of us."

Now perhaps it is better to believe in a human Christ than none at all. But this young fellow's trouble was quite typical, after all. His spiritual "metabolism" was off. He had large chunks of undigested theology lying around in his head. His head was far out ahead of his heart.

When you come upon a great creed like the Apostles' Creed, you cannot help but know that it was struck from the living heart of a living Church. Men first experienced the revolutionary truth about Jesus Christ. Then they sought to state it in understandable language. Hence our creeds. The event was first, then came the theological formulation of it. This is the true order of things in religion.

In fact that is the way it happend in the early Church. In the sixteenth chapter of Matthew's gospel we read how Jesus conversed with His disciples as they approached the region of Caesarea Philippi. He asked His disciples what men at large thought about Him. "Whom do men say that I am?" The reply varied. Some thought He was John the Baptist, others Elijah, and still others Jeremiah, or one of the other prophets. But now Jesus comes in close to the heart of His disciples. He probes them as to their own personal convictions about Him. They had spent long months in His inspiring company, had seen Him perform His wonderful miracles of healing and redemption. "But who do *you* say that I am?" He asks.

It was Simon Peter who gave the reply of the ages to the question of the ages: "And Simon Peter answered and said, Thou art the Christ, the Son of the living God."

Now notice that the Master does not whittle down this confession of Peter's concerning Himself. He approves it. Hear Him say, "Blessed art thou, Simon Bar-jona: for flesh and blood hath not revealed it unto thee, but my Father which is in heaven." This was more than a human reply to the question of Jesus. This was God bearing witness to Himself. As Joseph Parker once said, "Only a Christ could conceive a Christ."

When a noted skeptic once tauntingly said that he was divine in the same sense that Jesus is divine, he received a fitting answer from a believer. "Go right ahead," said the believer. "All you have to do is to get yourself crucified for a sacred cause, rise from the dead on the third day, and get the world to believe it!"

Jesus Christ Himself is the keystone in the arch of Christian faith. If we stand firmly at this point, we are firm everywhere. But if we are uncertain at this point, the whole arch of faith collapses.

> On Christ the solid rock I stand,
> All other ground is sinking sand.

But in what does this divinity, or better yet, the deity of Jesus Christ consist? How can you and I know that He is really divine? How can the assurance of the great radiant believers of the ages become ours? Oh, to be able to say with John Henry Jowett, writing from his deathbed to a fellow minister: "You and I have preached a great gospel. But Jesus Christ is greater than anything we have said about Him!" Let us seek honestly and humbly to answer this question of Jesus' identity for ourselves.

First of all, as one reads the holy and sacred scriptures, he becomes aware that Jesus Christ bore a unique and filial relationship to God. This is what we might call His God-ward side: "Thou art the Christ, the Son of the living God." These words could not be spoken about a merely human being. In His relationship to Almighty God as His Father, Jesus Christ is absolutely and utterly unique.

I recall how, as a college student, I went to a radiant Christian with my theological problems about Jesus — do we not all have them sooner or later? Said this trusted friend, "Don't make such hard work out of your faith in Christ. Just let Him reveal Himself to you. Believe that God has poured more of Himself into Jesus than into any other man that ever lived." As the years have passed, I have come to see the reasonableness of this counsel.

Jesus never forced his greatness upon anyone. Think, for instance, of that beautiful statement in Revelation 3:20: "Behold, I stand at the door [your heart's door], and knock: if any man hear my voice, and open the door, I will come in." His presence among those first disciples of His had all the glory of a sublime revelation. He was like a precious diamond, with its facets flashing in every direction — and yet not all at once, but in accordance with their capacity to see. And "see" Him they eventually did. In fact, one of them wrote down what he saw for the ages to come. Wrote Peter, "For we have not followed cunningly devised fables, when we made known unto you the power and coming of our Lord Jesus Christ, but were eyewitnesses of his majesty" (II Peter 1:16).

> What we have seen and felt,
> With confidence we tell.

Even a pagan the like of Napoleon Bonaparte was led to say, "Jesus Christ is more than man." You and I are not required to be trained theologians in order to lay hold of the truth that is in Christ Jesus, but only to be humbly receptive. After all, He never said, "Explain Me." His command was and is "Follow Me."

Daniel Webster was once queried as to his belief in the divinity of Christ. He was asked by a minister of his day, "Mr. Webster, can you comprehend how Jesus Christ could be both God and man?" "No, sir," replied Webster, "I cannot comprehend it. If I could comprehend Him, He would be no greater than I am. In fact, such is my sense of sinfulness before Him, and such is my knowledge of my own incapacity to recover myself, that I feel I need a superhuman Saviour." The great Webster spoke for many of us.

To the inquiring Philip Jesus said, "he that hath seen me hath seen the Father" (John 14:9). And to all of His disciples He said, "No man cometh unto the Father but by me" (John 14:6).

Sooner or later, that is where all of us must come out in our thinking about Jesus Christ. In a way in which we cannot humanly comprehend, He bears a unique and filial relationship to God. "Thou art the Christ, the Son of the living God." He is God Himself come in the flesh! (John 1:14)

His divinity is also found in what He said and taught. We have only a part of that marvelous teaching in our New Testament. But we have enough to make out the main outline of it. Briefly, He taught that God is a loving Heavenly Father who cares for all and each of us; that man bears the image and likeness of the divine, and that he is a "creature born for a revelation." He taught that man, as the child of God, has an infinite and a divine destiny, but that he has wandered away from his Father; that the way to return and enter the gate leading into the Kingdom of Light is repentance and faith. He believed that the Kingdom of God can come near to earth through devoted and dedicated men who are willing to deny themselves and to follow Him. He taught that He is the way to God. Those who listened to Him were led to say that He spoke as never man spoke. They sensed in Him and His words an authority that was unique. He Himself said that His words were spirit and life.

Jesus Christ never wrote a book or preached a formal sermon. His voice was never recorded on tape. But those who heard Him speak, recognized in what He said, the accent of the Holy Ghost.

Some of you may be acquainted with an incident concerning General Lew Wallace. The noted infidel, Colonel Ingersol, suggested to Lew Wallace that he write a book seeking to disprove the divineness of Christ. But in the process of constructing his book, Lew Wallace found himself facing the unaccountable Man. The more he studied His life and character, the more he was convinced that He was more than a man among men. At long length he came out where so many others have come out through the ages, at the feet of Jesus, saying like the centurion at the crucifixion: "Verily, this Man was the Son of God!" And the book which Lew Wallace wrote turned out to be *Ben Hur*, with its powerful testimony concerning the life and teaching of our Lord.

Let us go on to say now that Jesus' divinity lay in His command over the human heart. As none other, He knew what was in man.

Napoleon Bonaparte was a magnetic leader of men.

And yet, toward the end of his life he readily admitted that although Jesus depended only on love, millions through the centuries would die for Him. The unique ability of Jesus to understand the cravings and hungers of the human heart is illustrated in the words of a beloved gospel hymn:

No one ever cared for me like Jesus.
There's no other friend so kind as He;
No one else could take the sin and darkness from me,
O how much He cared for me.

—C. F. *Weigle*

Dostoevski, the Russian novelist, tells of a vision he once had. He found himself in a little country church with a large group of worshiping peasants about him. All at once it seemed a man came up from behind and stood beside him. He did not turn toward this man, but somehow he felt that the man was Christ. As he made an effort and turned to look on the man, he saw His face to be remarkably like every man's face. He wore clothes like those of the peasants around him.

There is a sense in which Jesus is kin to all of us. After all, He was the Son of Man. He was tempted in all respects as we are, and yet without sin (Hebrews 4:15). He knows the hard drag of the world on our hearts. He understands the turbulence we often feel in our souls. He is acquainted with the fears, the doubts and the despairs that plague us. How else could He be the one and only Mediator between God and man?

In fact, sometimes I am tempted to think that it is not so much the divine side as the *human* side of our Lord that bothers me. It is not the theology about Jesus, for that can be so impeccable, so abstract, so neatly logical. No, it is the ethics of the divine self disclosure — the actual living out of the teaching of Jesus — that challenges me the most. For see, the Great Confession of our Lord is followed by His

Great Commission! It is so easy to argue about the divinity of Jesus and so hard to live it out as He commanded us to do.

You say you have difficulty believing in the deity of Jesus? Then I suggest that you begin with His human side. Just try, for one day, to obey His simple command for you to be loving, pure, kind, honest and gentle. Try being a Christian at home, at school, in your social circle. Undertake to observe for even one day, His teaching with regard to the Golden Rule. If you will do this honestly and humbly, I believe that you will come out at the place where Peter and the other disciples came out at Caesarea Philippi: at the feet of your Lord, saying as they did, "Thou art the Christ, the Son of the living God." You cannot *really* know the "human" side of Jesus without being led into the great deeps of His character and nature.

Some years ago, when it was suggested that a Gothic Chapel for worship be erected at Chicago University, a devout elderly professor was overheard to remark that he was all for the Gothic Chapel, providing that they had some Gothic religion to put into it!

The Lord Jesus humbled Himself, and became "in fashion as a man" (Philippians 2:8). His divinity lay in His unique and startling command over the human heart and mind. He understands us as none other ever can.

Let us yet add this other word. Surely the deity of our Lord is to be found in His utter sovereignty when it comes to the ultimate issues of life and death, time and eternity. "All power," He says, "is given unto me in heaven and in earth" (Matthew 28:18).

As He quiets the storm on the lake, His disciples in the ship with Him exclaim, "What manner of man is this, that even the winds and the sea obey him!" (Matthew 8:27). He was Lord over nature.

Those miracles of His that sometimes bother you were not wrought for display. They arose out of His infinite compassion for those in need. They were the veritable sign that the Kingdom of God had come among men. He removed the veil from the face of mystery, took the sting out of death, and wrested victory from the grave. And even as we look through Him into the face of God the Father, even so He looks beyond His Cross into the glory of Easter dawn. Said He, "No one takes it [His life] from me, but I lay it down of my own accord. I have power to lay it down and I have power to take it again" (John 10:18). Not even death, the last enemy, could stand before Him.

One Sunday afternoon in the city of Rome, I stood looking over the gaunt frame of the Roman Colosseum where the early Christians had gone to their martyrdom. I tried to picture what had happened there in that terrible but glorious first century of the Christian era. I tried to imagine Nero tossing his petal into the arena and the great crowds crying, "The Christians to the lions." I could almost hear the jubilant singing of those first martyrs as they walked into the arena. Nothing, absolutely nothing could separate them from the love of God, which is in Jesus Christ (Romans 8).

It is this same conviction about the *livingness* of our Lord that makes us rise instinctively to our feet when Handel's great Hallelujah Chorus from *The Messiah* is sung. We hear the words, "King of Kings, and Lord of Lords," and what else can we do but reverently stand?

Dr. Joseph Sizoo told of talking to an elderly Korean woman who had suffered much from hunger and exposure during the time of war. This radiant Christian woman, whose faith had brought her through, said to him rather quaintly but meaningfully, "Thank you, America, for sending us food and clothes; but thank you most of all for sending us Jesus!"

Yes, Christ is divine in bringing us God the Father. He is divine and unique in His matchless teaching. He is divine in His power over our human hearts. He is divine in His victory over sin, death, and the grave.

What more can one say? What a Friend! What a Hope for a broken, distraught world. In the words of P. P. Bliss's beloved hymn:

Hallelujah! What a Saviour!

10 I BELIEVE IN THE HOLY GHOST

"He breathed on them, and said unto them, Receive ye the Holy Ghost."   (*John* 20:22)

WE IN OUR day have become increasingly unsure and uncertain with regard to the subject of the Holy Spirit. We resemble the disciples at Ephesus to whom Paul came. Sensing a lackluster quality in their lives, he asked them if they had received the Holy Spirit when they first believed. Their reply is amazing. "We have never even heard that there is a Holy Spirit."

To be sure, we know that the statement is in the Creed. On occasion we stand up in church and say, "I believe in the Holy Ghost."   But how deeply do we hold this belief? Are we not much more apt to say under our breath as it were, "Actually, I believe in an eloquent and learned pulpit, in church finance, in clever organization and large congregations, and in cultivating influential people!" Talk about the Holy Spirit seems like a vestigial remnant out of the long past. It is part of the unctuous and solemn phraseology of the church. We are perhaps like the little boy who came home from church one day and asked his mother what the people meant when they said, "I believe in the holy cats!"

But let us never forget it. To the first Christians, the Holy Spirit was real. For them, belief in the Holy Spirit was no magic incantation or superstition. The Holy Spirit was the veritable working of God Himself in their midst.

When, after His Resurrection, Jesus met with His defeated and sorrowful disciples in the Upper Room, He did not begin by saying to them, "Buck up, now." Nor did He tell them to go back to work. Our Lord Jesus put first things first. We read, rather, that He breathed on them the very Life of God, and told them to *receive* the gift of the Holy Ghost. Like stranded ships after the tide comes in, so these men were lifted out of the mud flats of impotence into a life of victory.

Now, that is what we need, isn't it? That is what you and I need! Believe me, there is power in this teaching of the Holy Spirit, and the Christian must not miss it. The subject opens out on a number of considerations we might well bear in mind.

Only the Holy Spirit can inspire vital, life-giving conviction in our souls. In Luther's phrase, "The believing man hath the Holy Ghost." We simply cannot push or scramble our way into a life-giving, sustaining faith. The Holy Spirit is a gift to be received, and only God can bestow it. Actually, we never begin to use the wonderful resources of our minds aright until Christ breathes His spirit upon us, until He releases His saving truth within us.

We can have God's life on His terms. We need to read again and again the wonderful story of the descent of the Spirit on the Day of Pentecost as it is recorded for us in the second chapter of the Acts. This man, Peter, who formerly denied his Lord, now stands straight and upright, and preaches one of the great sermons of all time. He rehearses the mighty acts of God culminating in the life, death and Resurrection of Jesus Christ. He makes it very plain to the unbelieving multitude that this One whom they had crucified, was raised up by God the Father. In the words of Karl Barth, "The resurrection is God's *Yes* to man's *No*." At the close of the service, no one crowded around the preacher to tell him how much they had enjoyed his sermon. This Man whom God made both Lord and Christ can be received only through repentance and faith. When unbelievers asked — having been pricked in their hearts — what they must do to be saved, Peter had the answer, the same answer that holds true for us today. He tells them to repent and to be baptized in the name of Jesus Christ for the forgiveness of sins, and that they would *then* receive the gift of the Holy Ghost (Acts 2:38).

It is the Holy Spirit, as the very life of God in the soul of the believer, who gives conviction.

When I was a little boy, one of my chores was to bring in the kindling wood for my mother. I recall how she would take this little bundle of thin sticks, and perhaps some bark from a tree, and light a match to it. Once the fire was kindled, everything else took flame. It was the tinder that set all else afire. Many of us will recall the lines of the old hymn:

> Revive us again, fill each heart with thy love;
> Let each soul be rekindled with fire from above.

The Holy Spirit in the heart of the believer is like throwing an electric switch in a dark room. He lights up everything. He makes dead creeds come alive. He releases power!

Again, we need the plenary inspiration of the Holy Spirit to gird us with power for the work God has assigned us. That is, we need the kind of power that doesn't peter out. Once we receive His power — and it must be received — we cease to be limited cisterns and become channels of spiritual power. Far too much contemporary Christianity is tired, run down at the heels, out of sorts. It doesn't leap and shout for joy. It lacks the New Testament imprimatur. It simply is not authentic.

The modern Church seems ecclesiastically over-organized and spiritually undernourished. When we are up against a problem in our day, we appoint a committee to see what can be humanly done about it. In the early Church they held a prayer meeting and called down the solution from on high. Authentic Christianity has always known that power belongs to God. "We have a supernatural task" said Dr. A. J. Gordon, "and we must have supernatural power to accomplish it."

During my Boston ministry, I was acquainted with a man by the name of Sargeant Bill Henderson. Big Bill, as we called him, had had a spiritual experience of great depth and intensity. Christ had literally snatched him out of a life of failure. After his conversion he dedicated his life to the cause of leading others into the experience that was his. And while he had never been to college or graduate school, he possessed a rare and intuitive knowledge of what it meant to be a Christian. He bore in mind that Jesus commanded the disciples to tarry until they were endowed with power, before they attempted to bear witness. Oftentimes I would walk through Boston Common, which incidentally was Big Bill's parish, and find him sitting meditatively on a park bench. When asked what he was doing, he would reply, "I am just being filled. I am waiting on the Lord. I am readying myself to bear testimony."

That is the New Testament teaching on the Holy Spirit. We are to be literally in-filled with the life of God. Dr. E. Stanley Jones, one of the radiant Christian witnesses of our generation, has said that he never takes a circuitous route when it comes to the matter of spiritual power. He goes direct to the Divine Source.

For another thing, only the Holy Spirit can offer us sure guidance and leading in the matter of ecumenical fellowship and dialogue. When you look at the divine blueprint revealed in the New Testament, you are convinced that the Kingdom of God cannot come through human cleverness and scheming. It can only be received. Only the Holy Spirit can create true and authentic Christian fellowship and togetherness. The early Christians designated themselves as simply "the brethren."

The danger of our day in seeking church unity is that we are so apt to begin on the outer periphery, and then work toward the center. The proper procedure is the exact opposite: namely, beginning at the center, with the living Christ Himself, and then working out to the periphery. The true church is a Spirit-filled community of souls.

Anyone watching the contemporary church scene knows that we will not become truly united around a set of by-laws, a liturgy however lovely, or above all through theological compromise. Look again at the blueprint in Acts: "And all that believed were together, and had all things common" (Acts 2:44). This is to really know the meaning of the words of the benediction, "the communion of the Holy Spirit."

At a meeting on church unity, a member of the United Brethren fellowship is supposed to have said, "In heaven, all men will be United Brethren." Whereupon a member of the Friends Society replied, "But if we are going to be United Brethren in heaven, we could at least begin by being Friends here on earth!"

I myself believe that the Church of the Living God lives in the heart of all those who love and serve the crucified and risen Lord. Where the Spirit of the Lord is, *there* is the Church.

True Christian unity is the achievement, not of men, but of God.

Consider also, that the Holy Spirit alone has power to breathe *the comfort of Christ* into our souls. The Holy Ghost is God's almighty arm about us in time of bereavement, trial and testing. That word "comfort" is not a saccharine word. It means literally to be strong with God: *con fortis.*

It was Jesus Himself who received the promise of the Comforter from the Father and passed it along to His believing disciples. What thrilling chapters those are in the gospel of St. John which tell us about the coming of the Comforter (John 14-16). Read them for yourself and be greatly inspired and uplifted. Jesus left His disciples in the body, only to return to them in the Person of the Holy Spirit. This Holy One, He said, would guide us into all truth, and supply all our needs. He would be with us forever because He would be in us.

The Bible also assures us that the presence of the Holy Spirit in the believing heart is none other than a down payment of eternal life itself (II Corinthians 1:22). In other words, the Christian already lives in the age to come. Already the powers of the eternal world descend upon the believer. Von Hugel, the famous German theologian, once defined the Holy Spirit as "an ever-flowing interior plenitude." It is the Holy Spirit, the presence of the Living Christ, who turns sorrow into joy, death into life, age into youth. An elderly radiant Christian was overheard to say that it was the Holy Spirit who put his shoulders back!

An invalid member of a church I once served told me in confidence of her fear of death. This fear seemed to grip her like a vise. Day and night it preyed upon her mind. She wanted so much to be rid of it and to claim the infinite riches of the Christian faith. As we talked, I opened my Bible to the eighth chapter of Romans and read: "The law of the Spirit of life in Christ Jesus hath made me free from the law of sin and death" (Romans 8:2). When it dawned upon her mind that the law of the Spirit of life in Christ was infinitely more powerful than any other law could be, especially the law of sin and of death — when she realized that the acceptance of the crucified and risen Lord frees the believer from all fear of death, then she was liberated from her fear. Death became an open door into life eternal. In a word, death moved out of her heart and Life moved in!

By way of a brief summary then, let us say: The Holy Spirit alone inspires solid, life-giving conviction within us. He alone can gird us with unlimited power for the tasks we face in this baffling hour. He alone can inspire into being the sense of the Church, catholic and apostolic. He it is who is our comfort and our stronghold in life and death. Then we can sing:

> Send forth thy Spirit, O Lord, our God eternal,
> And let the face of the earth be renewed, Alleluia!
> Come, Thou, Spirit, Heavenly,
> Expand our hearts with faith in Thy Holy name,
> And grant us Thy love and Thy mercy, O Lord,
> Thy peace everlasting!

11 THE TIME IS NOW

"But this I say, brethren, the time is short."
(*I Corinthians* 7:29)

ONE OF THE finest sayings of Ralph Waldo Emerson has to do with the value of time. "One of the illusions," says he, "is that the present hour is not the critical, decisive hour. Write it on your heart, that every day is the best day of the year." And he continues, "No man has learned anything rightly, until he knows that *every day is Doomsday.*"

That in essence, is the meaning of Biblical Christian living. It is buying up the time, measuring it over against eternity, stamping the Cross on each moment before it passes. It is "eternity fixing the conception of a single hour."

Consider the urgency of this saying of St. Paul's in I Corinthians 7:29: "But this I say, brethren, the time is short." Those first Christians felt that the very end of the ages had come upon them. They lived with a sense of crisis. As far as this world, at least, was concerned, the time was short!

Occasionally, people observing the large crowds of retired and elderly persons going to church here in Florida will say that they are "cramming for their finals!" The observation is not quite accurate. What has happened is that many of these people have lived long enough to realize the preciousness of time. They quite literally "buy it up." In the wise words of the psalmist, they number their days that they might apply their hearts unto wisdom (Psalm 90). A great Greek philosopher spoke of time as "the moving image of eternity." If there are some worthwhile things we still want to do in this life, then we had better get at them.

And that holds true for all of us, regardless of our age bracket. The time is now. Every day is Doomsday.

Stephen Grellett has left us some words to guide us. Said he: "I expect to pass through this world but once. Any good thing, therefore, that I can do, or any kindness I can show to any fellow human being, let me do it now. Let me not defer nor neglect it, for I shall not pass this way again."[1]

If we could realize the brevity of time, there would be some revolutionary consequences in our manner and way of living.

I, for one, would want to go out and look at the beauty God has placed in this world as I have never looked at it before. I would open not only my eyes, but my mind and heart to take it all in.

That remarkable woman, Helen Keller, once wrote an article for the *Atlantic Monthly* which she entitled, "Three Days to See." I have never forgotten it. It might be a salutary thing, she suggested, if all of us were stricken deaf and blind for a few days of our lives. The entailing darkness and silence would teach us the lessons of gratitude and appreciation. As Jesus long ago said, "Having eyes they see not, and ears they hear not." We fail to take in the bounty and beauty all around us. What would this great soul want to see if she had but three days of vision?

[1] Amos Lundquist, *Lives That Glorify God* (Philadelphia: Fortress Press, 1953), p. 307.

Helen Keller tells us that, first of all, she would call her dearest friends together — the ones who have made life worth living for her — and look deeply into their faces — and hearts. In fact, she wonders if we "seeing people" could describe at all accurately the faces of five of our close friends. How well could you pass that test?

Then too, she would want to see the face of a little child and to look into the loyal trusting eyes of her Scottie and Great Dane dogs who have meant so much to her. After a walk through the wonder of the woods she would pray for the glory of a sunset. Yes, and then the glory of "the magnificent panorama of light with which the sun awakens the sleeping earth" — a sunrise! "Oh, the things that I should see if I had the power of sight — for just three days!" For those of us with dull eyes and slumbering senses, Helen Keller writes some pointed counsel when she says: "I who am blind, can give one hint to those who see: Use your eyes as if tomorrow you would be stricken blind." There you have it! "Live 'as if' — the time is short."

Again, if I possessed this crisis-sense of time, I should have a deeper, more compassionate insight into the lives of my fellowmen. I would begin now to see them for what they really are — children of God, like myself, in various stages of development, all of them needing the encouragement and understanding I might give. In this matter of our human relationships, the time is short! Disraeli, who knew so well the taunts of unkind men because of race prejudice, said, "Life is too short to be little."

When I took the time to thank a teacher for the good she had done our children, she made a quite characteristic reply: "Your word of appreciation means more than you know. We get a lot of criticism in our work, but very little thanks." Why are we so niggardly about expressing the gratitude we must often feel?

The poet Whittier once wrote a poem he entitled "Forgiveness." In it he expressed the thought that he would not wish to face his Maker with a heart full of grudges. We might well memorize his words and take them seriously to heart.

> My heart was heavy, for its trust had been
>   Abused, its kindness answered with foul wrong;
> So, turning gloomily from my fellow-men,
>   One summer Sabbath day I strolled among
> The green mounds of the village burial-place;
>   Where, pondering how all human love and hate
>   Find one sad level; and how, soon or late,
> Wronged and wrongdoer, each with meekened face,
>   And cold hands folded over a still heart,
> Pass the green threshold of our common grace.
>   Whither all footsteps tend, whence one depart,
> Awed for myself, and pitying my race,
>   Our common sorrow, like a mighty wave,
>   Swept all my pride away, and trembling I forgave!
> —*John Greenleaf Whittier*

To love is to live.

If my days were rather suddenly foreshortened, I would also realize that I have some "make-up" work to do. You and I can live such selfish little lives in so great and needy a world as ours.

While he was cutting my hair one day, my young barber friend told me what was happening to his wife. She was becoming pessimistic and warped in her outlook. I asked him if she attended a Christian church. He replied in the negative. Said he, "I guess that is the trouble with her. She has lost her sense of spiritual vision and everything seems blurred for her." She, and he too, needed to be part of a Christian fellowship which could impart meaning and challenge and significance to their lives.

A young serviceman returning from the Second World War remarked that never again would the cause of Christian missions seem insignificant to him. He had seen first-hand the result of the faithful witness of Christian mission-aries. He had seen Christian natives risk their lives for American soldiers. Formerly he had filled in only one side of his church envelope — the side marked "Home Expenses." Now he would put at least an equivalent amount in the side marked "Our Christian World Mission."

It simply is not enough for us to have our names on a church membership list! We must take an active, vital part in publishing the glad tidings of Jesus, while we can. Why speak of evangelism if I have never seriously attempted to lead a soul to Christ? Why refer solemnly to Christian World Missions if the hunger and lostness of millions leaves me unmoved? What right have I to pray, "Thy Kingdom come, Thy will be done on earth," if I have done nothing to help fulfill the command of Jesus? Or, why speak of Christian Social Action if simple need passes before my door unheeded? Many people in our time are bemoaning the alarming statistics that have to do with juvenile de-linquency, but they have yet to share in extending to youth what Ella Lyman Cabot referred to as "temptations to right-doing." Did not our Lord say, "Why call ye me Lord, Lord, and do not the things which I say?" (Luke 6:46).

The late Dr. George Truett of Dallas was a man of rare fervor and power in his evangelistic ministry. He fairly glowed with a passion for souls. Early in his ministry he cultivated the friendship of a dedicated young man with whom he would occasionally go hunting. On one of these expeditions he accidentally shot his friend, and the sor-row of this accident remained with him all through his life. However, George Truett was wise enough to lay his sorrow on the altar of Christian Service. From now on, he must live for the two of them — his friend and himself. And this he did as few men could have done it. He literally moved thousands toward Jesus Christ and the Kingdom. To shake his hand was a benediction. For George Truett time was short! Now was the time of decision. Would to God we all had this sense of urgency, whether laymen or ministers!

While still a young man, David Livingstone, the great missionary, made a vow. "I propose" said he, "to put no significance by anything apart from its relationship to the Kingdom of God."

Sir Alfred Zimmern, renowned historian, once said that the greatest obstacle in the way of building a lasting, Christian peace in the world was the "small-scale individual." It is later than we think. The time is short.

Another thing: if a crisis sense of the meaning of time dawned upon me, I would somehow want things to be right between God and my own soul. The words of the Apostle would dawn on me with fresh emphasis: "Behold, now is the appointed time; behold, now is the day of salvation" (II Corinthians 6:2).

I confess that when I first entered the Christian ministry I used to look with amusement at the red letter sign on the gospel tent at the edge of our community: "Prepare to meet thy God, O Israel." These roving evangelists were queer people with weird ideas in their heads about the end of the world, I thought! They were always trying to frighten people into repentance with their rantings. They were the lunatic fringe of the Church.

Well, that was what I said and thought, *then.* Today I am no longer intolerant toward these people. They teach an element of truth that we need to heed. If time is of the essence, then God knocks on my stubborn heart saying, "Are you ready to meet Me? Are you living a life deserving of the great gift of eternal life?"

Yes, I am done making light of "fox hole" religion. The great Roman, Seneca, said: "Let me live every day as though it were to be my last." And none other than our

Lord Jesus Himself teaches us to have our loins girt, and our lamps trimmed, and to be as servants to whom much has been entrusted, ready for their Lord's return (Luke 12:35-40).

Recently I met a man who was noticeably profane. As we talked, he used some very precious words, but in the wrong context. I introduced myself to him, told him of my work, and suggested that he might like to worship with us sometime. "Strangely enough," said this man, "my mind just never runs along that line. I just am not concerned about such things." For a moment I was about to back down and say nothing further. Why cast my "pearls before swine" (Matthew 7:6)? But then the thought came to me that this was a good time to bear a Christian witness. Surely this man was in need of it. And so I said to him, "Has it ever occurred to you that this life is not all, and that ultimately we must face our God and the prospect of life eternal? You say you never think of these things. I see many people on the edge of eternity and they *do* think of these matters. My friend" I went on, "what you and I think about God and life eternal is not as important as what God, the Heavenly Father, thinks about us." At least this man left in a pensive and thoughtful mood!

Only fools live this present little life without thought of God, eternity and the judgment! Jesus said so in His parable of the man with his bloated pride and his full barns: "Thou fool, this night thy soul shall be required of thee" (Luke 12:20). Actually, we have only today.

After the death of Mr. Daniel S. Ford, former editor of *The Youth Companion*, they found on his desk, much worn with frequent handling, the following poem. The words are a fitting epitome of a man who had done so much to lift the burdens of others and inspire the youth of his day:

The bread that bringeth strength I want to give,
The water pure that bids the thirsty live;
I want to help the fainting day by day;
I'm sure I shall not pass again this way.

I want to give the oil of joy for tears,
The faith to conquer crowding doubts and fears,
Beauty for ashes may I give alway;
I'm sure I shall not pass again this way.

I want to give good measure running o'er,
And into angry hearts I want to pour
The answer soft that turneth wrath away;
I'm sure I shall not pass again this way.

I want to give to others hope and faith,
I want to do all that the Master saith;
I want to live aright from day to day;
I'm sure I shall not pass again this way.

The time is short. We shall not pass again this way!

12 THE HEALING OF OUR TENSIONS

"Rest in the Lord, and wait patiently for him."
(Psalm 37:7)

DID YOU EVER have a little boy ask you to untie his shoe-strings when they got all snarled up? It is an interesting experience, to say the least! If you will let patience have its way, you will finally get the shoelaces unsnarled, and you will gain a lesson in patience and perseverance in doing it.

After one such little chap came to me the other day, it set me thinking of human beings and their problems, especially the problem of tension and stress, which takes such a terrific toll in modern life. Look at the list of our afflictions — high blood pressure, hearts prematurely played out, ruffled and irritable tempers! Said a young business executive to his pastor, "I'm so highstrung and irritable, both at home and at my place of business, that at times I am almost ashamed of myself." Dwight Lyman Moody used to say that he had more trouble with a man named Moody than with anyone else!

Sit down sometime and carefully read the 37th Psalm as a kind of creative exercise. Here was a man, very much like ourselves, all in a dither about world conditions and what he calls the "evil doer." And then, when he is at the

100

breaking point, Almighty God takes him by the hand and speaks to him, saying, "Don't be so fretful about the evil doer and the worker of iniquity. His days are numbered." Instead, what is he to do? He is to "trust in the Lord," to "delight himself in the Lord," to "commit his way unto the Lord." Above all, he is to "*rest* in the Lord" and wait patiently for Him. Ah, if only we could learn to do that! Then God would unfold our lives in harmony with His will for us, and tension would fold its tent like the Arabs, and silently steal away.

Not that we are to engage in a kind of escapism. God's will for us is not stagnation, but that we make that full and complete commitment of ourselves to Him that will bring us inner soul-rest. In Him we may find a calm center from which to live. As another has put it,

> The calm beauty of an ordered life,
> Whose very breathing is unworded praise.

And now — as with the little boy and the snarled shoe-strings — let us try and find a few places to get hold of in our quest for inner serenity.

Suppose we begin at the center. Nothing can so effectively remove the tensions that bother us as a firsthand experience of the renewing, cleansing grace of God. Nothing can so take the "kinks" out of us as a fresh experience of God's forgiveness, in which we realistically face ourselves and get right with both God and man. And do you know, sometimes I think that good, respectable people like ourselves need it the most!

Recently I noticed the calm, serene face of an elderly saint at a funeral service I was conducting. Like the sun piercing the clouds on a dark day was the face of this person. And as the great words of St. Paul in I Corinthians

15 were read, it was evident that she knew their meaning firsthand.

By way of contrast, here was a man who was sent by a psychiatrist to a clergyman. He said upon his arrival that he felt "all picked to pieces" and very much pushed around. He knew so much about himself, and yet so little! He was inwardly unhappy, divided, restless. And then, lovingly and understandingly, that minister guided him into an old-fashioned experience of conversion. The transition from self to God at the center of his life was made. Gradually he let go of his inner tensions and learned to "rest in the Lord." He rested in that which God had mercifully provided in Jesus Christ for his salvation. He took life abundant and eternal as a gift from the outstretched, pierced hand of Christ. The false props came down. For the first time the house of his life rested on firm foundations. Christ became his all in all. Now he had found his true self. He had discovered peace through God's forgiveness.

There is an oriental prayer which says, "O God, heal me at the center, and then let life come on." Dare to discover your true self in Christ! Let Him fill you to the full with His redeeming grace. When faith comes in, false fears depart. They cannot live in the same heart. "If any man be in Christ, he is a new creature" (II Corinthians 5:17).

Dr. Farmer, former organist at Harrow, once pleaded with a Salvation Army drummer not to beat his drum so hard. The beaming bandsman replied, "Lor' bless you Sir. Since I have been converted I am so happy I could bust the bloomin' thing!" Talk about the "expulsive power of a new affection!" That man had it.

Here is a further word closely allied with this first bit of counsel: Ask God to fill you with unfeigned love and good will for your fellowmen, and irritability will stop tying you into knots. We are speaking now of something very real; of a basic good will which only Christ can release in our hearts. Perhaps it is this horizontal relationship which is out of gear in your life.

Some time ago I had occasion to talk with a man whose heart was cankered with hatred and resentment. He felt that he had been shamefully used in a former business relationship, and perhaps he had. When he was warned that he himself would foot the bill for his resentment in terms of inner neurosis and anxiety, he readily agreed. And yet, he went his way unheeding, perhaps to end up an ulcer patient in a hospital. It has been said that the ulcer is the wound-stripe of our generation. Truly, ulcers are the result not of what we eat but of what is eating us!

The Gospel of Jesus Christ, with its teaching of mutual forgiveness and good will, is the sanest counsel ever given to mortal man. If there is a point of difference between you and your neighbor, so it teaches, then settle it. Get it over with. Don't let it fester into resentment and ill will. If we are at the church altar with a gift, and there is ill in our heart toward our brother, then we must first go and make things right, and then come and make our offering. What common sense this is! How utterly sane and sensible such teaching! "Let not the sun go down upon your wrath" (Ephesians 4:26). If you do, you will take it to bed with you, spend a sleepless night, and ultimately pay the bill in sickness of mind and body.

I sometimes think that if we ministers charged a fee for the counsel we are often asked to give, people would put it into practice more realistically. You see what I mean by this, do you not? People are so apt to say, "Well, that is the way ministers talk. We won't take it too seriously." And yet these same people will walk down the street to the office of a psychiatrist and pay a high fee for much the same advice!

In the long run, only Christ with His Gospel of love and forgiveness, can bring us healing. Christian love and good will flood the inner being with the glow of spiritual life, health, and strength. Resentments tie us into knots and kinks, and poison the innerspring of our lives.

Dr. Robert McCracken confesses that when he first came to Riverside Church in New York City, he had a difficult time. The constant crowds with their pushing and shoving on the street cars in the late afternoon wearied him no end. To be a strap-hanger on the subway and to smell garlic on the breath of persons of nationalities other than his own frankly irked him. He found himself seeking the counsel of another who had been living a long time in New York. This wise pastor admitted that he himself had faced the same problem. How to love "all sorts and conditions of men" in a polyglot environment — that was the problem. And the solution was forthcoming when a genuinely Christian attitude toward others was adopted. Said this counselor, "I found myself praying for these thousands of human beings round about me and crowding me on the subway, many of them with the same sorrows and troubles that I had. I found myself loving them in the great love of God." Then the weariness left.[1] Only redemptive love can win a victory like that. What is more, it can and will do it for us all.

There is only one thing to do with human beings, said a great soul, and that is to love them. And love, when it flows from a warm, Christian heart, relieves the high tension of daily living, and fills the heart with a new sense of

[1] Robert J. McCracken, *Questions People Ask* (New York: Harper & Row, 1951), p. 58.

peace and joy and strength. Only those who love really *live*.

Last, but not least, we need to get more of the hint of the eternal into our day-by-day living, and to do all things for the glory of God! There is nothing like this attitude to take the weariness and strain out of living. It is said that Raphael once wrote a significant word over the work of one of his students. That word was *amplius*! It means, Larger! Bigger! To pause occasionally during the day and say to yourself, "I am performing this task to the glory of God." It will challenge you to make your endeavors worthy of God's blessing. Too many of us are preoccupied with secondary matters of little moment. We need to get our lives back on the Kingdom pattern. The great composer, Bach, used to write the words "For the glory of God," over his compositions.

It is even possible to come to Florida and miss out on the really great things there are to enjoy here! Go out and look over the broad expanse of the waters of the Gulf of Mexico, and if you like plunge into its tangy depths! Take a look at a sunset in which the infinite Artist mixes all the colors of the spectrum, and then flings them on the canvas of a western sky for your enjoyment. Or look up into the Southern sky at night, and see the stars so close they almost seem to whisper to you. Take advantage of the opportunity to feel the warm heart of people who gather here from all over the world. Get the feel of what is going on in church on a Sunday morning as, in the company of a multitude of people like yourself, you call on the "Father of lights, with whom is no variableness, neither shadow of turning."

A tourist friend was telling me how he mentally photographs the natural beauty he finds in Florida — the Poinsettia in full bloom in December, the vast expanse of the ocean, the sky and the waters — the sight of an egret on the water's brim — and then mentally recalls them in the

wear and tear of things in his office back home. He says that
just to remember sets him free. Recall how the poet W. H.
Carruth described it:

> Like tides on a crescent sea-beach
> When the moon is new and thin,
> Into our hearts high yearnings
> Come welling and surging in.
> Come from the mystic ocean
> Whose rim no foot hath trod,
> Some of us call it Longing,
> And others call it God.

Bishop Fiske used to tell of the elderly Maine guide he
and a few of his friends employed during their vacation
time in the woods. This was during the summer when
William Jennings Bryan was making his last attempt at the
Presidency, and rock-ribbed Republican Maine was wor-
ried. At night they would sit about the campfire talking
things over. One of the men present was a geologist and
spoke of the age of the rocks. Another, a research physician,
spoke of the long, long evolution of life on our planet. Yet
another, an astronomer, mentioned the immeasurable dis-
tances of the stars glimmering in the sky. Sitting there and
taking all this in, was the old guide.

Soon he began to ask questions. Were the rocks really
so old? Were the stars so far away? Was the evolution of
life actually so long out of the past? When at last he got
it settled in his mind he heaved a sigh of relief. "I guess,"
he said, "it won't make a powerful lot of difference even if
William Jennings Bryan is elected president!"[2]

When the pressure of life threatens to be too much for
you, get a new experience of God's cleansing and redeeming love in your heart. Let the Almighty "strike His glory"

[2] Harry Emerson Fosdick, *The Power to See It Through* (New York:
Harper & Row, 1935), p. 130.

throughout your day. Love others in the great love of God. Put yourself utterly at the service of Christ and your fellowmen. Then you will come to know the meaning of this great comforting Psalm — "Rest in the Lord, and wait patiently for him . . . . Commit thy way unto the Lord; trust also in him; and he shall bring it to pass."

13 ARE YOU A DRIFTER?

"We ought, therefore, to pay the greatest attention to the truth that we have heard and not allow ourselves to drift away from it."

(*Hebrews* 2:1, Phillips Translation)

WHAT A SPIRITUALLY and morally rudderless generation ours has turned out to be! Evidences of this fact abound.

A financial empire, supposedly invulnerable, crashes and becomes a national scandal. An American actress who engages in tandem divorce, and is a disgrace to our nation both at home and abroad, is nevertheless idolized by millions. A young lad goes suddenly berserk and victimizes his entire family. The stock market on Wall Street strikes a new low for apparently no reason at all, except that of fear. Said one newspaper correspondent, "People are plain scared." The highest judicial body in the land rules 6-1 that it is no longer legal for school children of our land to repeat a simple non-sectarian prayer at the beginning of the day. We seem to be all sail and no anchors!

Now what is the reason for all of this? Why do we act on caprice rather than conviction and react to the challenges of our day with fear instead of faith? Is it not that we have lost our spiritual moorings, that the great moral bastions that anchored our forebears have lost their hold on us? Is it not that the mighty sheet-anchors of the soul that gripped our parents and grandparents are noticeably absent in our time?

Someone tapped a woman on the shoulder on a busy downtown street and said, "Pardon me, Madam, but your slip is showing." Spiritually speaking, is not that true of our age and time? Our "slip" is showing.

If you will open your Bible to the second chapter of the letter to the Hebrews, you will find a word which speaks directly to our modern lostness. Evidently the generation in which the author lived was as wobbly and uncertain as ours. We hear him say: "We ought, therefore, to pay the greatest attention to the truth that we have heard and not allow ourselves to drift away from it." In other words, he is saying beware lest you become a drifter!

When the writer of Hebrews speaks of "the things we have heard," he makes quite clear what he means. He is referring to the faith proclaimed by the Lord Himself, attested to by those who heard Him, and corroborated with signs and miracles and the outpouring of the Holy Spirit. What a faith indeed! "How shall we escape," he asks, "if we neglect so great salvation?" (Hebrews 2:3) The answer is, of course, *we shall not escape.* We ourselves choose the direction of our lives and, humanly speaking, we are the arbiters of our destiny.

Suppose that we be frank and honest with ourselves, and ask the rather blunt question, "*Am I a drifter?* Am I losing sight of the moral moorings of the faith? If I pursue my present course, where will it lead me?" Tragedy lies in the fact that so often the drift is imperceptible. Our "slip" is showing, and we do not realize it!

The late Ernest Hemingway was a portent of our generation. He was gifted, cocksure, outwardly self-sufficient. Not long before he died, some newspaper reporters visited him. Now the cocksureness was gone. The man was a mere shadow of his former self, and what is more, to all intents he had no spiritual resources to see him through.

Surely, then, here is a word we all need to heed: "We ought, therefore, to pay the greatest attention to the truth that we have heard and not allow ourselves to drift away from it."

But let us do far more than merely generalize. Let us have the courage to be specific. Here are a few test questions which will reveal how things are with us.

Are you drifting away from a life of vital communion with God through prayer? Surely it is axiomatic that prayerless lives cannot be God-conscious and God-girded lives.

By this is not meant that we need to be monks, spending the live-long day on our knees, sitting about with folded hands of resignation. Most of you are busy people, with jobs to do, children to provide for, and responsibilities to bear. Nevertheless, only through a life of conscious, deliberate communion with God in prayer — what Paul referred to as "unceasing prayer" — shall we hold our course aright. We need to keep the communication lines open between our souls and the Almighty Soul of the universe. Else we drift. It is nothing less than tragic to go through the day prayerless and unmindful of God's presence.

Here, as elsewhere, the example of our Lord Jesus Christ can help us. Recall the words He spoke at the tomb of Lazarus. Death and despair had settled upon that little home in Bethany. And now, see. We read in the eleventh chapter of John: "And Jesus lifted up his eyes, and said, Father, I thank thee that thou hast heard me: And I knew that thou hearest me always" (John 11:41, 42). Notice the word "*always.*" Our Saviour was strong in time of crisis because His life was utterly God-related. The dialogue between Father and Son was never broken. We are strong in time of crisis only if we have been faithful along the way.

In our parsonage in Minnesota, I can recall the occasions when the door to my father's study was shut. He had no "keep out" sign on his door, but we knew what he was doing. He was kneeling in the Divine Presence. He was getting his marching orders for the day. Said Emerson: "When I sit in that Presence, who shall dare to enter?" But when my father left his study, he carried the atmosphere of prayer into all the affairs of the day. So many of us in our day are powerless because we are prayerless. We have lost the sense of God's presence in our lives. We have become drifters.

> One ship drives east and another west,
>   While the selfsame breezes blow;
> 'Tis the set of the sail and not the gale
>   That bids them where to go.
> Like winds of the air are the ways of fate,
>   And we journey along through life;
> 'Tis the set of the soul that decides the goal,
>   And not the storm or the strife.
>   —*Ella Wheeler Wilcox*

Here now is another rather pointed question with regard to this matter of drifting. Has the Bible, as the Word of God, lost its command over your life? Do you take time — or rather *make* time — to read the Bible and to meditate on its glorious promises? Is it chart and compass for your life? Personally, I do not see how any person can live a victorious Christian life who has not the substance of the Holy Scriptures in the very marrow of his bones. The head of our Federal Bureau of Investigation, J. Edgar Hoover, once remarked that because of the lack of Biblical precept, many Americans seem spiritually berserk and rudderless in our day. We have deserted the Book of our fathers. We have thrown our spiritual chart and compass overboard and are adrift in a storm.

Suppose you open your Bible to the fourth chapter of

Matthew's gospel and see how the Lord Jesus met temptation in the wilderness. Basically, He faced the same temptations which we face in our day. He was tempted of Satan
to bow down and worship wordly power, to feed on the
vain husks of materialism rather than on the Word of God.
Notice also that for each temptation, Jesus had an answer
straight from the Sacred Writings. Each time He answered
the tempter with the words, "It is written." In fact, He
returned to His native Galilee from His wilderness testings
in the power of the Spirit. He was stronger, not weaker, for
His ordeal. Blessed is the man, the woman, the youth, who
in the wilderness of modern doubt and temptation can
answer, "It is written!"

In his book, *I Found God in Soviet Russia,* John Noble
tells of the Lutheran pastor who was a prisoner in a communist prison camp in Siberia, where he himself was incar-
cerated. The prisoners used to meet together in secret in
a passageway of the mines. They had no hymn books or
Bibles among them. However, this man of God could quote
from memory whole chapters of the Bible. Like the Psalmist
he could say, "Thy word have I hid in my heart." He had
stored up the very bread of life in his soul, and now he was
sharing it with his fellow prisoners in their time of need.

It might also be asked: are you one of the many who
are drifting away from the practice and custom of public
worship on the Lord's Day? Do you know the joy of asso-
ciating yourself with those who worship the Lord in the
beauty of holiness? Do these words of William Cowper
speak to you:

> Jesus, where'er Thy people meet,
>   There they behold Thy mercy seat;
> Where'er they seek Thee, Thou art found,
>   And every place is hallowed ground?

A man who had drifted away from church once told me
how it all happened. At first, he would feel very guilty

as he heard the sound of the church bell on Sunday morning. Gradually, the sound of the bells with their summons, dimmed on his hearing, until finally he no longer heard them. He had become a drifter.

A man dropped in on one of our services of worship on one occasion, with a typical "you've got to show me" attitude. He was thoroughly cynical in his attitude. That Sunday, however, the Lord had put into my heart just the right message for that man. My text read as follows: Jesus, "as His custom was, . . . went into the synagogue on the sabbath day" (Luke 4:16). Now notice that public divine worship was a settled custom with Jesus. The highest and holiest Soul who ever trod this earth was faithful when it came to the worship of God. He did not attempt to separate himself from the "turbid ebb and flow of humanity" when it came to church attendance, or to complain that there are too many "hypocrites" in the church. In other words, He, who knew God as none other has ever known Him, felt the need to worship. All of this I sought to point out in my message that day. This man told me later on, what had happened to him in church that Sunday. He became thoroughly ashamed of himself. He was cut down to size. He knew himself to be a mortal creature, dependent on the grace of God, and he went home to make amends. Now he no longer says to his children, "You go to church," but rather, "Let us go to church together."

I have never known a strong and well-rounded Christian who did not make a definite place in his life for worship on the Lord's Day. As John Wesley put it, "There are no solitary Christians."

We have one more question to ask. This is actually the question on which the others crucially depend. Are you on speaking terms with Jesus Christ? Do you know Him as a daily present Companion, Guide and Master in your life? Or are you a drifter in this respect?

It is when we lose the sense of His presence that prayer becomes drudgery, the Bible a fairytale, worship a mockery, and God an unreality. The writer of the letter to the Hebrews makes it abundantly clear that the great salvation of which he speaks is ours only in Christ Jesus. A bit later on in the letter he gives us that great heartening word that Jesus Christ is "the same yesterday, today, and forever" (Hebrews 13:8). Surely, we shall not escape if we neglect our relationship to Jesus Christ. It is through Jesus Christ that we believe in God.

In his great poem, "The Hound of Heaven," Francis Thompson tells us his story. He attempts vainly to flee from the great pursuing Presence. Finally he is tracked down by the Heavenly Hound, and hears words addressed to him: "All things betray thee who betrayest Me!" May not this be the experience of some of us? Talk about "displaced persons!" Literally thousands of them walk the streets in our modern American cities. We need the assurance of a great Christian of former days, who said, "I have gotten me Christ, and Christ has gotten me the victory."

Some of us have had the rare experience of crossing the Atlantic Ocean on a great liner. On one such trip I remember the joy of seeing the famous White Cliffs of Dover, of which the Britons sang so much during the days of war. At last we were coming into port. We had been a week at sea, and during that time had never gotten a glimpse of our captain. Nevertheless, he was on board all the time, faithfully keeping watch at the helm. And now he was bringing us safely into port.

Is not that a parable of what the Christian life should really be? The vessel of our life seems far adrift on seas sometimes very stormy. We cannot see the outcome of events which seem so disturbing. The Christian, however, is at peace, because he has the Great Captain of his salvation aboard the vessel of his life.

There is a story of a backwoods preacher who had had hardly a day of formal education in his life, but who nevertheless had a vital transforming Christian experience to share. One day he was summoned before an examining board to determine the state of his credentials. He was asked what evidence he could give for the deity of Jesus Christ. That backwoods preacher sat stunned and helpless before such a question. He did not quite know how to answer it. His kindly examiner changed the question somewhat. "Can you tell us why you believe that Jesus Christ is divine?" The question struck tinder. Now this man was on his feet, arms extended, as he cried out, "How do I know He is divine? Bless your heart, He saved my soul, and I love Him!"

Have you this knowledge? How about these anchors of the soul, so far as your life is concerned? Glance again at them: prayer, the Bible, divine worship, a firsthand experimental knowledge of Christ as Lord and Saviour. In days to come you will be needing these anchors. By all means, lay hold on them while you can, and they will give you a fresh grip on life. Surely, this writer of long ago is speaking directly to all of us when he says: "We ought, therefore, to pay the greatest attention to the truth that we have heard, and not allow ourselves to drift away from it."

Why be a drifter?

14 LEARN TO PRAY LIKE THIS

"Lord, teach us to pray."   (*Luke* 11:1)

THE LATE Joseph Fort Newton in his autobiography *River of Years* tells of coming home on one occasion and hearing his mother at prayer. His mother, a rare saint, had appointed times during the day in which she engaged in communion with God. She would read a verse of Scripture, sing the verse of a hymn, and then kneel and pray. On this occasion, her son overheard her praying for him. She was lifting him up before God and holding him there, asking divine guidance upon his youthful life. We do not wonder that not long afterward, he decided to enter the Christian ministry.

It was in much the same manner that the disciples of Jesus came upon their Lord in the act of prayer. What a light shone on His uplifted face! With what poignancy they became aware of their own spiritual poverty! At least they had the good sense to wait until he had done with his devotions before they made their request — surely the greatest any mortal can make: "Lord, teach us to pray, as John also taught his disciples" (Luke 11:1).

In answer to their request, Jesus gave them the prayer of the ages, in which He distilled the larger dimensions of what it means to commune with God. We call it the

Lord's Prayer. Actually, it is the disciples' prayer, for it was His gift to them. What is more, the prayer was never meant to be a crutch for the lazy, but a pattern of approach for the earnest seeker. The Master did not say, "Pray using these exact words" but "After this manner, pray." We might put it thus: "Learn to pray like this."

This prayer which is recorded at length in the sixth chapter of St. Matthew is what we might refer to as a model prayer. Some time ago I visited a new housing development in a section of our city. Here was a model house which might be inspected by potential buyers. In this house you could see the architect's idea of what he conceived to be a home. It was not meant as a design to be copied in detail, but a pattern which potential buyers could keep in mind as they planned their own homes.

This, I believe, is what Jesus had in mind when He said, "After this manner pray" (Matthew 6:9). What mighty spiritual laws undergird this prayer! What power there is in it. What a shame that so often we merely *say* this prayer, parrot-like. Familiarity has dulled our appreciation of its greatness. In my early ministry I knew a humble but devout farmer who used to say, "Preacher, everything we — and our world — need may be found in this prayer."

There is of course nothing we frail mortals can add to the prayer of Jesus! We have yet to even touch the hem of the garment of His mighty words. Did not Tintoretto fling down his brush and say, "After all, who can paint the ocean?" The prayer then is a blueprint, a chart and compass, to guide us in our quest for God. There are certain great tidal movements in it, like those of a Beethoven symphony, or like the motifs of a Wagnerian opera.

In this chapter we shall be very much on our knees at the feet of Jesus. My good friend Dr. Samuel Lindsay used to say that while Jesus never taught men to preach, He *did* teach them to pray. The Master knew what He was doing. He knew how easily we humans become discouraged and give up. That is why He tells us that "men ought always to pray, and not to faint."

An atheist has been defined as a man without invisible means of support. When you and I are prayerless, we are rutted in our own little human resources — and how small they are! When we open our hearts to God in prayer, then He is with us and we cannot fail. Dwight Lyman Moody used to say that prayer is just opening the heart and letting Christ come in.

Look now at a few of the statements, some of them petitions, in this greatest of all prayers.

First of all our Lord utters a great ascription of praise to God, when He says, "Our Father who art in heaven, hallowed be thy name." He begins at the beginning. He begins where the Bible begins, with its statement, "In the beginning, God . . ." (Genesis 1:1). In these words Jesus makes the most supreme assertion ever uttered by human lips: Our Father who art . . . . He never argues the existence of God. He assumes it. He never wastes time trying to "prove" the existence of God almighty. He brings us God. As Joseph Parker of City Temple, London, used to say, only a Christ could conceive a Christ!

No one can doubt that the best thinking of our day is veering in the direction Jesus pointed out so long ago. Find a great thinker and you will find a great conception of God, as Creator, Redeemer and Sustainer of the universe. Sir James Jeans, noted physicist, has said: "The universe begins to look more like a great thought than like a great machine." And he continues, "Mind no longer appears as an accidental intruder into the realm of matter; we ought rather to hail it as the creator and governor."[1]

[1] Quoted in *Rufus Jones Speaks to Our Time,* Harry Emerson Fosdick, ed. (New York: The Macmillan Company, 1961), p. 33.

William Newton Clarke, in his classic *Outline of Christian Theology* is in agreement with the great physicist. Nothing is more certain, he wrote, than that science in its maturity will affirm one spiritual cause for the universe. Mark well these words of the great theologian: "In the march of science, the recognition of the Universal Mind is the next legitimate stage" (page 117). Wordsworth put it thus in "Tintern Abbey":

> And I have felt a great Presence
> That disturbs me with the joy of
> Elevated thought.

But our Lord Jesus, when He prayed, looked beyond a mere "Mind" and "Presence" to One who was a personal Father and the Sovereign God of the universe. Hear Him: "And this is life eternal, that they might know thee the only true God, and Jesus Christ, whom thou hast sent" (John 17:3).

You who read these words must have made the great ascription of faith in some rare moment of insight. We may be somewhat reticent about sharing such experiences, but nevertheless in our time of need, God was *there*.

A friend of mine who is not ostensibly religious, once confided to me his experience. Ill and lonely in a great city hospital and looking into the face of possible death, he became aware of the Divine Presence. And never since has he doubted the reality of God Almighty, the great I AM THAT I AM.

The prayer now moves from the vertical out into a horizontal dimension. It visits the desert places of the world's need. The Lord Jesus bids His disciples make the most daring petition ever uttered: "Thy Kingdom come. Thy will be done in earth, as it is in heaven" (Matthew 6:10). In these words the

    . . . whole round earth is every way,
    Bound by golden chains about the feet of God,

as Tennyson put it.

How often you and I, and thousands of other Christians, have made this petition! How seldom we pause to think what it is we are asking! If we did, it might shock us. For this petition deals the deathblow to all provincial, niggardly thought and prayer. With one mighty stroke it sweeps from the board all lesser kingdoms of man, the kingdoms based on race, color, nationality, materialistic theories. In actuality there is only one Kingdom, and that is the "everlasting kingdom of our Lord and Saviour Jesus Christ" (II Peter 1:11). All other kingdoms are temporal.

The noted art critic and writer John Ruskin used to say that if a man doesn't want the Kingdom to come, he should not pray for it. But if he does, he will not only pray for it, but work for it!

The noted student of history, Arnold Toynbee, insists that our age will be remembered, not so much for its horrible crimes or its brilliant scientific discoveries. It will be remembered, most of all, for the fact that, for the first time since the dawn of history, we have begun to realize that the fruits of civilization belong alike to all mankind.

It goes without saying that when our praying is for the glory of God, it should make large demands! Christians are people who live, work and pray that the will and reign of Almighty God may encompass the whole earth. The world for them is a sphere for kingdom building. Christ has commanded "as in heaven, so on earth," and shames us out of our tepid, picayunish praying. We must be done once and for all with small thinking, small praying, small living. Said William Carey: "Expect great things from God!"

A bishop of the Methodist Church[2] once told of a visit

[2] Gerald Kennedy, *God's Good News* (New York: Harper & Row, 1955), p. 101.

he made to a Christian village in Africa. He was invited to preach at an outdoor service. Seated before him were several thousand Christian neophytes, eager to hear the good news of the Gospel. At the close of the sermon the African preacher beckoned to one of his church officers nearby to lead in prayer. What a prayer it was! The native interpreter kept informing the visitor as to what was being said in the prayer. Now the petitioner was praying for Christians in America, that they might be fit instruments of God for the coming of His Kingdom. Now he was praying for Christians throughout the British Commonwealth of Nations. Again, he was praying for Christians of Asia and Africa, especially for those who were hard beset by paganism, persecution and communism. The prayer literally *girdled the earth*. What that African Christian was saying in his prayer was this: "Thy Kingdom come on earth, O Lord!" This is what might be called a soul-stretching prayer! It must be uttered from yearning hearts if it is to reach heaven.

Verily Lord, teach us to pray like this!

The next petition of the prayer walks the plain everyday places of our human need and toil with its words, "Give us this day our daily bread. And forgive us our debts, as we forgive our debtors" (Matthew 6:11, 12).

We are to remember that Jesus was raised in a carpenter's home, that He worked in a carpenter's shop, and that He knew what it meant to do a hard day's work. He who knew not where to lay His head during His public ministry, must have known the meaning of poverty in some of its forms. Notice that He does not teach His disciples to pray for luxuries, but for the necessities of every day. Recall how He multiplied the loaves on several occasions, until there was enough for all, and that He asked that the crumbs be gathered up that nothing be lost. (It has never been hard for me, reared as I was in a large minister's family, to believe this miracle of the multiplication of loaves. My Christian mother must have performed this miracle daily! Else how would she ever have fed her large brood?)

In my ministry here in St. Petersburg, I spend considerable time talking with people in their advanced years about their needs. These people wish to be sure that they will have a roof over their heads, food enough to eat, medical care during illness, and decent Christian burial at death. Call it bread for the body if you wish — but there it is! Give us bread for the day!

But the Lord Jesus was not satisfied that we have bread for the body only. We must also have bread for the soul lest we perish. Yes, give us this day our daily bread, *and* forgive us our debts — that is, our sins, our failures, even as we forgive our debtors. This is the imperishable bread of the Spirit without which a man cannot truly live. When our Lord instituted the sacred Supper, He took bread and broke it in the midst of His disciples. At Emmaus He was known in the breaking of the bread (Luke 24:35). And He spoke of Himself as the living Bread from heaven (John 6:35, 51).

The great heart of Jesus knew that in order to forgive his fellow humans, a man must first of all himself be forgiven. A woman came to see me whose heart was filled with ill will and resentment. Her friends and relatives had dealt unfairly with her, so she said. I suggested to her that although I could not offer her the gift of forgiveness, there was One who could. Together we prayed. Sincerely and earnestly she besought God to forgive her for her pathetic resentments. Thereupon she rose from her knees, a new light on her face, to say, "A great load has been lifted from my heart. Now I can go out and forgive others!"

Once we learn to pray this kind of prayer, we become channels of God's forgiving grace. This spirit of forgiving love is tragically needed in our modern society, rankling as it is with misunderstanding between man and man, race and race, nation and nation, class and class. And the place to begin is with ourselves. My friend, earnestly pray this prayer as you have never prayed it before: "O God, forgive me that I may be forgiving! Make me a channel of Thy saving grace!" Truly did the Master pray, "And lead us not into temptation, but deliver us from evil" (Luke 11:4). Or, as Dr. J. B. Phillips translates these words, "And keep us *clear* of temptation."

We have noticed that the prayer Jesus gave His disciples begins on the note of God's majesty. It then moves out horizontally into the places of human need, out where people toil and suffer and die. Our Lord Jesus would have us remember the hungry and the destitute and the lonely. He would have us think of the teen-ager who finds it difficult to live in our modern society. He would have us think of the American serviceman who swelters in the jungles of Viet Nam. He would have us think of children who languish in broken homes. What a vast need there is for the prayer of Jesus uttered from a yearning, loving heart! After traversing the valley of human need, the prayer now ends on the repeated note of the majesty of God and the Eternal Kingdom: "For thine is the kingdom, and the power, and the glory, for ever."

These closing words of the Lord's Prayer are not in the original prayer Jesus gave. How could they be, insomuch as He had not yet undergone His great passion of suffering and victory? The words were added by His followers in the early Christian fellowship in tribute to their living, reigning, glorified Lord. The words are a soaring, singing doxology, a veritable burst of praise, like the sound of trumpets, and the roll of drums.

> The Head that once was crowned with thorns,
> Is crowned with glory now.
> —*Thomas Kelly*

How inspiring to think that for almost twenty centuries of Christian history the Church has worshiped in these words: "For thine is the kingdom . . . for ever!" The prayer is offered to the risen Christ.

Occasionally at a marriage service the Lord's Prayer is sung to the beautiful arrangement of Malotte. As it is sung, two young people kneel reverently at the altar, uniting their hearts in prayer to the One who alone can join them in sacred, holy matrimony. How that kind of marriage is needed in our day! Occasionally, while officiating at such a marriage, I experience a feeling of wonderment and awe as the words are sung. And I have seen many a young couple rise from their knees, tears in their eyes, knowing that only this is the kind of marriage that no man *can put asunder!*

Dr. David Smith, noted Bible commentator, tells us that the prayer Jesus gave His disciples is essentially a *morning* prayer.[3] The disciples had followed their Lord to His hillside oratory, witnessed His devotion, and now when He had ceased, the sun was rising over the Judean hills. It was morning. As the disciples go their way again from this sacred retreat, it must have been morning, joyous morning, in their hearts. "His Kingdom," said Luther, "is forever."

"Our Father who art in heaven" — God lives!

"Thy Kingdom come!" — May that Kingdom be in my heart, and may I be its instrument.

"Give us bread!" — Bread for the body, and for the soul.

[3] *Commentary on the Gospels, Matthew* (New York: Doubleday & Co., 1928), p. 115.

"Forgive us our debts as we forgive our debtors." — Men identify His disciples by the love they express.

"Deliver us from evil." — Keep us always loving.

"For Thine is the Kingdom and the power, and the glory,

Forever!"

15 TRY GIVING THANKS

"Now consider this, ye that forget God . . . . Whoso
offereth praise glorifieth me: and to him that ordereth his conversation aright will I show the salvation of God." (*Psalm* 50:22, 23)

HANS CHRISTIAN ADAMSON, senior military observer, was
one of the gallant crew of Eddie Rickenbacker who all
drifted on a rubber raft for more than three weeks on the
Pacific. Let him tell us in his own words what this ordeal
did for him in changing his attitude toward life and above
all in inspiring the spirit of thankfulness in his heart.

> Just now I am trying to get a new outlook on life.
> On a Friday afternoon we were spotted by a Marine
> Corps plane and were picked up later. You cannot
> imagine the prayers of thanksgiving we offered. While
> drifting was a horrible experience, something wonder-
> ful has come of it. I have found a nearness to our
> Creator which I have never known before, and I am
> certain that this new feeling is going to deeply affect
> all our lives in the future.[1]

Dale Carnegie tells of a conversation he had with
Captain Eddie Rickenbacker concerning this same experi-

[1] Wallace Fridy, *Lamp Unto My Feet* (Nashville: Abingdon Press, 1952),
p. 119.

126

ence. When the latter was asked what he learned from it he replied that if anyone has fresh water enough to drink, and food to eat, he should never complain!

Sometimes it takes a crisis experience to awaken us to the need for being thankful. We take the blessings of life from day to day for granted. We become selfish and introverted in our attitude. William James, famous Harvard psychologist, once said that, the greatest discovery of modern times lay in the fact that our lives can be completely altered through a change of attitude.

Our national mood at present is hardly one of gratitude. Far too many of us look upon life with a "spoilt boy" attitude. Life hasn't given us the "break" we deserved. The very expression of our faces belies our religious professions. A well-known lecturer on religious subjects sometimes begins by asking how many of the people in his audience are Christians. After they have raised their hands, he says to them, "You say that you are Christians. Why don't you notify your faces?"

After a Sunday school teacher had sought to teach her children the true meaning of the parable of the Good Samaritan, she asked them what they had learned from this lesson. Said one little fellow, "When I am in trouble my neighbor should help me out!"

In the fiftieth Psalm, God speaks to this surly, selfish mood. Surely these are words which constitute a "primer" on the subject of thanksgiving: "Consider this, ye that forget God . . . . Whoso offereth praise glorifieth me: and to him that ordereth his conversation aright will I show the salvation of God."

A woman of morbid outlook was one day sharing her many complaints with a radiant Christian friend. After her long Miserere of complaint, she was asked, "Have you ever tried thanking God for your blessings? If you will do this you will find out that you have much more to be thankful for than to complain about." This advice was accepted and practiced, and the direction of a life was changed. D.L. Moody used to tell about an old man who lived on Grumble Street. Then he had a true experience of the grace of God in his heart. Said he, "I moved from Grumble Street to Thanksgiving Street, and have lived there ever since."

Turn again to these wonderful words of the fiftieth Psalm. The psalmist is, as it were, putting words in God's mouth. The Almighty is telling us that if we offer Him praise and order our lives aright, He will show His marvelous salvation unto us. This is the remedy that we need for many of our modern ills, especially, ills of an emotional nature. We need to stop griping and start thanking. We need to get a different outlook on life. We need to weed out of our vocabulary all negative and ungrateful words. We need to glorify God in our conversation with one another. Then, and only then, can God visit us with the gift of healing and salvation.

All the way through the ministry of Jesus Christ, we hear His words, "Father, I thank Thee." Even with the Cross in sight, He nevertheless can praise and thank His Father.

Let us look a little more deeply into this attitude of thankfulness.

For one thing, we should offer praise to Almighty God because He is the Lord, the All Righteous and Holy One, the Father of our spirits. "The chief end of man," wrote our fathers in their catechism, "is to glorify God and to enjoy Him forever." In other words, God is worthy to be praised.

Daily we walk beneath an over-arching providence. We are pensioners on an infinite bounty. Unfortunately, we tend to forget this in our so-called day of science, technology and automation. We are so apt to worship human cleverness rather than the God and Creator who has breathed the very breath of life into our souls. We worship the creature rather than the Creator. There is a story about a Sufi woman saint, who was running with a pail of water in one hand, and a torch in the other. When she was asked what she was doing, she replied, "I want to burn up heaven with a torch, then put out hell with water, so that men will not love God for fear of punishment or hope of reward, but will love him for Himself."[2] The Christian loves and worships and praises God primarily not for what He gives, but for what He is in Himself.

Graven on a hassock in an old English church are words which we might well take to heart in this day: *Think — Thank.*

One finds this spirit of humility and thanksgiving in the heart of the truly great thinkers of our day. Little self-sufficient, proud men cannot praise and thank the Almighty. They are too full of themselves! It is far different with a noted scientist like Sir Joseph Thomson. Man cannot look upon the azure canopy of heaven, says this great scientist, nor contemplate the wonders of creation, without realizing that he is face to face with infinity. At such a time a man can only speak the words of the psalmist when he says, "What is man, that thou art mindful of him? and the son of man, that thou visitest him." To such a man, and to such a thinker, the universe is not a cold, blind mechanism, but an organism, literally indwelt with the glory and the power and the wisdom of an infinite Creator. The farther the advance of science, the more the scientist is led to say, if he reflects deeply, "Great are the works of the Lord!"

To many a person it needs to be said, "Get your mind off the clamor of your wants and be stayed upon the loving kindness and greatness of the Lord." If we will change our

[2] E. Stanley Jones, *Victorious Living* (Nashville: Abingdon Press, 1963), p. 252.

attitude from complaint to praise, a new sense of the true meaning of life will dawn upon us.

An elderly woman was overheard to say that when she could not sleep well at night, she had a practice of saying, "Thank You, Father." This, in spite of her inability to sleep. Before long she would sink into satisfying, rewarding sleep. That might be worthwhile counsel for those of us who are insomniacs. Said Thomas à Kempis, "All I need and long for is in Thee."

How thankful we should be also, for the loyalty and fellowship of God's believing, faithful people.

An elderly physician I once knew had a way of saying, "You know, there are still a lot of good people around." This, in spite of unfortunate experiences he may have had with some of his patients. Over the door of a restaurant in our city are written the words: "The best people in the world go in and out of these doors."

Recall how, in the nineteenth chapter of the first book of Kings, the prophet Elijah was down in the mouth and discouraged. He complained to God that he was the only faithful person left on the scene. "I, only I, am left," said this tragic man; "and now they seek to take away my life!" Someone has quipped that the poor man had become an "I specialist!" He was soundly rebuked by the Lord and informed that there were always the seven thousand who were faithful.

Let me give a personal testimony at this point. If ever I get discouraged in the Lord's work, I remember the many people who have been such a blessing in my ministry over the years. What a wonderful army, this fellowship of the committed! When I enter my pulpit on a Sunday morning, I know that the heart of the people is with me. I can feel the support and prayers of my many friends. There are many people present who are as eager and concerned for God's cause as I am. Many of them may be better Christians. The same has been true in our radio ministry. One hears from such wonderful people. Yes, indeed, God has His seven thousand.

On Easter Monday, 1953, the pastors of Bavaria unveiled in the church in Flossenburg, Germany, a tablet with this simple inscription:

> Dietrich Bonhoeffer, a witness of Jesus Christ among his brethren. Born February 4, 1906. Died April 9, 1945.

The whole world, almost, has become acquainted with the ministry of this wonderful man to his fellow prisoners in a Nazi concentration camp. One of his friends, an English officer, was overheard to say that wherever Bonhoeffer might be, he always spread an atmosphere of happiness and joy abroad. He possessed a spirit of profound gratitude for the fact he was alive, even in a concentration camp. God was always near and real to him. At the very last he was executed by special order of the infamous Nazi, Heinrich Himmler. As he was led away to the gallows, these were his last words: "This is the end. But for me it is the beginning of life."[3]

Great souls like this make thanksgiving very real to us. One of the great values of church attendance lies in the inculcation of this spirit of praise and thanksgiving in our hearts. Surely nothing can be more inspiring than to rise with a congregation of like-minded people and join in a hymn like that of Joachim Neander:

> Praise to the Lord, the Almighty, the King of creation!
> O my soul, praise Him for He is thy health and salvation!
> All ye who hear, now to His temple draw near.
> Join Him in glad adoration.

[3] Dietrich Bonhoeffer, *Life Together* (New York: Harper & Row, 1954), p. 13.

When Lyman Beecher was pastor of Park Street Church in Boston many years ago, he was asked the secret of his successful ministry. He replied, "On Sunday morning I preach to my congregation, and all week long there are 500 people or more who go out preaching the message."

We here in America should also be personally and collectively grateful for the fact that, in spite of the trials and trepidations of the moment, the foundations of our great republic still remain intact. I recall a little bootblack in Lisbon, Portugal, who told me how much he would like to emigrate to America. His fondest dream was to be able to come here to live.

Please do not think me the victim of a false optimism. Barnacles of neglect cling to the Ship of State here in America. The great Ship is adrift in perilous waters. We are living in trying and testing times. This is one of those eras in which anything can happen, depending upon our response to the challenge of the hour. All this let us readily admit. Nevertheless, I believe that underneath all the turmoil, the underlying principles and foundations that founded this nation of ours still endure. We can rediscover them in our time and build a future on them. This is the day in which we should look to the rock whence we are hewn and to the pit whence we were digged. Well did Longfellow write in his "Building of the Ship":

> In what a forge and what a heat
> Were cast the anchors of our hope!

But on the other side of freedom lies responsibility. We dare not forget that.

One evening while visiting in the quaint town of Killarney, Ireland, I left our hotel and went down to a little variety shop. A motherly little woman of mature years waited on me. She was just the kind of person any boy or girl would be proud to have as his grandmother. After I had bought my knickknack and handed her an American dollar bill, she looked at it very carefully, and then held it up for me to see. And this little Irish woman gave an American tourist one of the finest sermons he had ever heard. Said she: "What beautiful words you Americans have inscribed on your money: 'In God We Trust.' As long as you remember these words and obey them, yours will be a great nation. But if ever the time comes when you forget them, then God help you."

What a time to remember that this nation of ours was founded by a little Pilgrim band who sought freedom to worship God. It was this desire that brought them here. A lot of Americans are forgetting that in our day. Their first homes in the wilderness went up side by side with their meeting houses of worship.

These American pioneers of ours also insisted on respect for the individual. They believed in the sublime worth of the human soul. In the sight of God, a man was a man, whatever his color, class or nationality.

And then let us not forget that in spite of the ferment and unrest of the hour progress in our human relationships has been made. One hears a number of people talking about the "good old days." They have a way of looking back over their shoulders into the past. But which of us, if we were honest, would want to return to them?

While in Geneva, Switzerland, we visited the League of Nations building which now houses the European branch of the United Nations. Granted, of course, that this human organization has many shortcomings. It is, to be sure, a human institution. But how much better for the heads of nations to sit down, and talk things out, rather than shoot them out! Here one meets people from all over the world, of all languages, races, and nations. One instinctively feels that the heart of humanity is yearning for peace and understanding. "Come, let us reason together, saith the Lord." Is not that the challenge of the great Lord of history to the peoples of our day? As Christians, we share with God in the great creative travail of bringing His many sons into glory.

In "Remembrance Rock," Carl Sandburg pictures Judge Windom as a man great in thought and rich in years. The Judge has what he calls a "Remembrance Rock" in the very center of his yard. Around this rock he has gathered a bit of dust from all sorts of shrines, among them Plymouth Rock, Valley Forge, the bloody battlefields of France. This precious dust he has brought hither about his rock. The old Judge likes to sit there and meditate concerning the hard, thorny road over which his great nation of America has come.

The important thing to remember about Judge Windom, however, is that he is faced *forward*. He has no use for people who insist that the great days of history are over. Remembrance Rock he regards as a steppingstone into something greater. His monument is a living monument. The best days for America, and the world at large, are yet to be.

Well do I remember a day out of my early ministry in the great state of South Dakota. Calvin Coolidge, then President of the United States, was to speak at the site of our State College at Brookings. A great campanile had been installed on the grounds of the college and the President was to bring the dedicatory address for the occasion. Somehow we managed to slog our way through the muddy roads, until a great multitude of us were gathered together. I do not recall all that Calvin Coolidge said on this occasion. But one word of his has remained with me through the years, a word which heartens me as I think of the present and future of our beloved land. "America," said the President, "is still a young nation. Her greatest days lie before her.

And our part as Christians and as citizens, is to help build that greater future."

As the many small town businessmen and farmers made their way back to their homes, they felt they had a part in the shaping of a great future.

Let us stop our complaining and start praising God! The winter of our discontent can give way to the spring and summer of thanksgiving. Praise the Lord because He is worthy to be praised! Yes, praise Him for His mighty acts, above all for His great act of salvation in our Lord Jesus Christ. Let us praise God also. as did Dietrich Bonhoeffer, for the privilege of serving in the army of God's loyal people. As Christians, we have the most precious fellowship on earth. It is the best thing this side of heaven. And then, my fellow Americans, never forget that the great foundations of our Republic must remain intact. Be it ours to rediscover them, and build a greater future on them.

"Whosoever offereth praise, glorifieth me!"

Try thanking God!

16 JESUS CHRIST IS ALIVE!

"But now is Christ risen from the dead."

(I Corinthians 15:20)

IT HAS BEEN said that, we do not believe in the Resurrection because we can prove it, but that we try to prove it because we cannot help believing it. That is, we do not conjure up theories to prove the fact of personal immortality. We are witnesses to the trustworthiness of what Darwin referred to as "the grand instinct." David Smith, Bible commentator, termed the Resurrection of Jesus Christ the surest event in human history.

The New Testament is a powerful testimonial to the Resurrection of Jesus Christ. We do not come across any "maybe's" or "ifs" as we read this inspiring literature. What we find instead is a record and a testimony. The great Paul who had encountered the Living Christ on Damascus Road gathered up the meaning of the Resurrection in the great fifteenth chapter of I Corinthians. The certainty of this fact is summed up in a few brief words: "But now is Christ risen from the dead!" (I Corinthians 15:20).

Suppose then that we point out a few of the revolutionary consequences that follow in the wake of the mightiest event of history.

First of all there is the testimony of the *Church mili-*

tant and triumphant, itself a monument to the Resurrection of her Lord. The Christian Church was founded on the fact of Jesus' mighty victory over death. As Dr. C. H. Dodd, famous British student of early Christianity put it, "The one incontestible result of the life, death, and resurrection of Jesus Christ is the emergence of the Christian Church." Early Christianity had but one message. It is reiterated all through the glorious passages of the New Testament: "Jesus and the Resurrection."

Something wonderful happened at that first Easter which lifted the gates of empires off their hinges and turned the stream of civilization into new channels. Something which gave a new date to time and a new dimension to the human soul. Something that changed a company of timid and hesitant men into a group of heroes and martyrs for the faith. Indeed, something happened which has kept the Church alive in the world as a supreme power for good, for over nineteen hundred years. No myth nor phantasy can accomplish that — only an event and a reality.

Along with the emergence of the Christian Church there was born also the Lord's Day, the first day of the week, on which Christians gather to worship the risen Christ. A queer little old lady of my acquaintance used to pester me with regard to the fact of the Lord's Day. Somehow I could not get her out of the Old Testament with its Sabbath Day! Read the four gospels with their triumphant conclusions, get the drift of the letters of Paul, and you cannot but be convinced that Christ is the end of the law, including the matter of ordinances and special days, for the believer. The law is fulfilled in grace. The brittle, regulatory ordinances of a former day gave way to the good news of a present and living Lord. And the Sabbath gives way to Sunday, or the Christian Lord's Day. In fact, the Church with her Lord's Day and her two main sacraments of Baptism and the Lord's Supper, are a crowning monu-

ment to the fact that our Lord Jesus Christ could not be
holden by death. This Christian Lord's Day of ours is
meant to fling its glory over all the days of the week, until
every day is a Lord's Day.

A visitor in New York City once told of his experience
after attending a service of worship at the Fifth Avenue
Presbyterian Church, when Dr. J. H. Jowett was minister.
Walking in Central Park, he noticed the faces of the people
he met. Some faces looked hard, arrogant and careworn.
It was obvious that these people had not been in church.
Then he met a stream of people altogether different. They
seemed to have escaped the prisonhouse of care. In their
eyes there was a glow of victory. These were the people
who had heard John Henry Jowett proclaim the glorious
message of Jesus and the Resurrection.

Yes, the church itself is a monument to the crowning
event of history, namely, that Jesus conquered death!

The fact that Jesus Christ is alive also means the end
of cynicism and defeat for the believing Christian, while
it makes of life a sacred trust and magnificent adventure.

For most of us, the Resurrection of Christ simmers down
pretty much to this: If Christ be *not* risen from the dead,
then nothing much matters! Then sow your wild oats, put
your passions in the saddle and let them ride you. Then
eat, drink and be merry, for tomorrow we die. We often use
the terms ethics and morality in a very loose manner, as
though they were complete in themselves. The fact is, these
terms become worthless abstractions apart from faith in the
immortality of the soul. If this life be all, if there be no
judgment in which the secrets of all hearts shall be disclosed,
if there be no Infinite Accountant who will one day weigh
the good and the ill, if there be no eternity for which to
prepare, then *what matters?* Why all the tears and self
denial and sacrifice that go into the building of strong

Christian character! Life becomes a thing "full of sound and fury, signifying nothing."

But if, as our divine faith teaches and as humanity's greatest hearts have believed, this life is a training ground and vestibule for larger, ampler life, and if we must sometime look into the searching eyes of that One who gave Himself for us, the just for the unjust, then *that* is different. Our so-called ethics and morality become implemented with spiritual significance. Then immortality is not only a gift, but in a very real sense, an achievement. And only "they who strive mightily shall possess it!"

Said the famous Roman, Cicero, "I quit life as if it were an inn and not a home. The soul is about to set out for a better country." And according to Robert Browning, "Now is for dogs and apes; man has forever!"

This present generation, so sadly munching the stale rinds of futility, needs nothing so much as an invasion of life-giving, deathless faith. Lorado Taft has warned us that art, literature and music must get more of the "hint of eternity" into them. Else they shall bear no significance for the present, and no carrying power for the future. You can gauge the spirit of an age by the quality and nature of its art. Put it down to their wisdom and credit: the immortals created and the saints lived with their eyes on the horizons above! We in our day are not art-ful because we are not belief-ful. We are an age which worships idols, fashions trinkets — not monuments. "The hint of eternity" — how we do need it!

Minus that hint of eternity, even the witness of the Church palls and fails. Man is seen as a secular creature with no eternal destiny. Men begin to doubt that the leopard can change his spots and the Ethiopian his skin (Jeremiah 13:23). Missionary zeal and giving decline. The urge to better the lot of our fellowmen within our own country and abroad goes into decline. The Kingdom waits.

The redemptive urge forsakes preaching. And tell me please, how shall we go on contending for democracy, and face up to the brutal truculence of dictators, if man be only the vaunted plaything of a moment? How shall we Christians abolish the war monster which desecrates the human personality Christ has purchased with His blood? In the last resort, Easter means *God's evaluation of life*. A victorious and revolutionary faith can never end at the Cross. Verily, if in this life *only* we have hope of Christ, we are of all men most miserable! (I Corinthians 15:19). It is so!

But the Resurrection of Christ not only has to do with the emergence of the Christian Church and the end of personal defeat. Death itself is defeated and the last enemy has been overcome. Captivity itself is carried captive. Midnight gloom gives way to radiant morn. Christ Himself emerges the Universal Conquerer, with the keys of death and hell swinging at His girdle. Hearts that had grown despondent on Emmaus road now stand beside an empty tomb.

> The head that once was crowned with thorns,
> Is crowned with glory *now!*

Some years ago a man by the name of Marvin Black wrote a most unusual book entitled *The Pendulum Swings Back*. In this book he argued that taps has been sounded over the corpse of materialism. That our first-rate scientists are preaching that life is dynamic and not static. That strictly speaking, there is no such thing as matter, but that even the tiniest atom is a whirlpool of life and energy. Write it in large letters across the borderline of our best thinking — and living: *there is no death!*

Hear this truth uttered from the lips of the very Lord of life Himself: "I am the resurrection, and the life: he that believeth in me, though he were dead, yet shall he live: and whosoever liveth and believeth in me shall never die" (John 11:25, 26). He Himself *is* Resurrection, He *is* Life.

The famous aviator and author, Antoine de Saint-Exupery, in his amazing book, *Flight to Arris,* tells us how he was freed from a great illusion about life. Before he took up flying, his body seemed to be the solidest reality in his thinking. Like most men, he had spent a great deal of time on the flesh. Says he, "I had dressed it, bathed it, fed it, quenched its thirst. I had identified myself with this domesticated animal. I had taken it to the tailor, the surgeon, the barber. I had been happy with it, loved it. I said of it, 'This is me.'"

And then, quite of a sudden, this illusion faded out. The body took its rightful place in his thinking. It became a mere flunky in the service of his real self. Says he, "A diving plane stripped away the flesh." He ceased to identify his true self with the body of flesh and bones. He became lost in a larger life. He came to know that man is a spirit, who uses a body. After such an experience, he says, "The body which we have coddled and cared for, mistaking it for ourselves, drops like a wornout rag, of no further use."[1]

Now the remarkable thing for us to observe is that this startling discovery did not begin with Antoine de Saint-Exupery. This is what Jesus Christ and the great writers of the New Testament insisted upon almost twenty centuries ago. Paul stressed it constantly in his great chapter on the Resurrection (I Corinthians 15). This mortal must put on immortality, and this corruptible must put on incorruption. Christ has torn the mask from the face of death and set us free from fear. We are commanded not to sorrow as those who have no hope. Christian, yours is a Resurrection faith, a living Lord, who faced sin, death and the evils

[1]Quoted by Joseph Fort Newton in *Live, Love and Learn* (New York: Harper & Row, 1943), p. 142.

of the world, and laid these grim specters low. Life can become new for us! John Wesley used to say, "Our people die better."

Now, close this book and say inwardly to yourself, *"Jesus Christ is alive.* He lives in me by the power and presence of His Holy Spirit. Because He lives, I shall live also."

JESUS CHRIST IS ALIVE!

17 A LIVING FAITH AT WORK

> "For the kingdom of God does not mean food and drink but righteousness and peace and joy in the Holy Spirit." (*Romans* 14:17, RSV)

WHILE TOURING ENGLAND a few years ago, we came to Oxford on a Sunday afternoon and went out to Christ Church College, the Alma Mater of the great John Wesley. Here in the old library were the quaint tables and chairs, and the well fingered books bearing their silent testimony of centuries of scholarship and study. On the walls were pictures of some of the famous alumni of Christ Church. But near the entrance as we left, in a prominent position, was the picture which I most of all revered — that of John Wesley, himself. As you walk around the old campus, you have the feeling described in the hymn: "Brothers we are treading, where the saints have trod." The past came strangely alive.

For a long time now I have been living quite intimately with John Wesley's *Journal*. How Wesley ever managed to write his journal, spending as he did a good share of his life on horseback in all kinds of weather, I do not know. But the pages of the journal fairly scintillate with the record of God's dealings with his soul. He became a man whose religion was one of sheer joy. And what a record, the record of his life! Small wonder the historian, Greene,

stated that it was John Wesley who spared England the
terrors of the French Revolution. On one occasion he writes
of a visit to Epworth, the place where he was born and
where his father was once the incumbent minister. Wesley
was not permitted to preach in his father's pulpit. However,
this field preacher, so-called, was not easily put off. He re-
sorted to the strategy of having a helper, John Taylor, stand
at the door of the church at the close of the service and
announce that John Wesley would preach at six o'clock in
the churchyard. And so, come six o'clock, Wesley stood
on his father's tombstone and cried out the famous words of
Paul in Romans 14:17: "The kingdom of God is not meat
and drink; but righteousness, and peace, and joy in the Holy
Ghost."[1]

What we are concerned with in this chapter is not
the bare miscellanea of Wesley's life, that is, his birth, education, death, etc. These can be gotten from any encyclo-
pedia. He lived a long life, being born on June 17, 1703,
and living until the ripe age of 88 years. What we want
most of all to know is, What was the *secret* of such a life?
What made the man "tick"? Wherein lies his vast and vital
contribution to the whole life of the Christian enterprise?
You simply cannot coop a man like Wesley up in any sec-
tarian corner. He would not stay put for long. He himself
said, "The world is my parish," and what is more, he meant
it. John Wesley belongs to all of us, being one of God's
rare saints. Like all of God's great ones, there is something elusive about the man. He seems dateless, timeless,
indescribable. Here, however, are a few gleanings that come
to mind as one fingers the pages of his arresting journal.

He knew first-hand the need and the reality of the
New Birth. To be born once, even as Jesus told Nicodemus,
simply was not enough. The new birth was not a dead doc-

[1] *Journal,* entry for June 6, 1742.

trine, or a thing of mere words to Wesley, but something he knew firsthand, experimentally.

He knew so well how full the mind could be, and how empty the heart! In this respect he resembles some of the tragic secular existentialists of our day. This Oxford Don, John Wesley, was a Fellow of Lincoln College, and a master and teacher of the Classics. He was brilliant, learned, armed with the knowledge of the best schools of the day. He was hotheaded, proud and headstrong, as witness the failure of his missionary venture in Georgia.

He could not help but marvel at the fearlessness of the Moravians as they sang during the time of storm at sea, while he himself cowered in fear. This pre-Aldersgate Wesley was simply not ready to face death, to say nothing of life!

Returning to England after his experience in Georgia, he tells us in his *Journal* how he went very unwillingly one evening to a society in Aldersgate Street. While there he listened as someone was reading from Luther's Preface to the epistle to the Romans. Surely the words of John Wesley are a classic:

> About a quarter before nine, while he was describing the change which God works in the heart through faith in Christ, I felt my heart strangely warmed. I felt I did trust in Christ, Christ alone for salvation: And an assurance was given me that he had taken away my sins, even *mine*, and saved *me* from the law of sin and death.[2]

This was the life he had been seeking for all along, and which the most erudite professional and classical scholars could not offer him. Yes, this was it, a firsthand experience of the wondrous grace of God in Christ. Once and for all he joins himself to Christ as his personal Saviour

[2] *Journal*, May 14, 1738.

and Lord. This was not book learning, but living encounter with a real Person.

Yes, write it over against the life of John Wesley, and the lives of thousands of others who have learned the precious secret: "The Kingdom of Heaven is righteousness, peace and joy in the Holy Spirit."

So real and authentic is Wesley's firsthand experience of God's grace that when he was 51 years of age and in failing health, he wrote a suggested epitaph in case of his demise. It read as follows:

Here lieth the Body
of
JOHN WESLEY,
A Brand Plucked Out of the Burning;
Who Died of a Consumption in the Fifty-First Year
of His Age,
Not Leaving, After His Debts are Paid,
Ten Pounds Behind Him;
Praying,
God Be Merciful to Me, an Unprofitable Servant![3]

Again, pause to consider that this man, who was dubbed a "Methodist" because he was punctilious and methodical to a fault in his observance of his religion, yet is the man who set the church of his day to *singing*. Along with his brother Charles, he wrote some of the great hymns of our Christian faith. After all, the Kingdom of Heaven is joy! Why shouldn't he sing! He lubricated, as it were, the cold, rationalistic structure of the religion of his day with the oil of joy. The Christian faith is an exultant faith because it extols Jesus Christ. Just imagine our church hymnals without these words of John Wesley:

Love divine, all loves excelling,
Joy of heaven to earth come down.

[3] *Journal*, Nov. 26, 1753.

> Till we cast our crowns before Him,
> Lost in wonder, love and praise.

Or without the hymn of his brother, Charles:

> O for a thousand tongues to sing
> My great Redeemer's praise!

On one occasion he comes to a preaching appointment at a place named Wem, only to find that no one much was expecting him. The weather was exceedingly inclement, and he took refuge in the market-house of the city. Instead of bemoaning the fact that no one was present he breaks out into singing. By and by people crept into the house in the market place — first just a few, and then by the hundreds. "The power of God," he wrote in his *Journal* later, "was so present among them, that I believe many forgot the storm."[4]

Wesley's was a religion that could sing! And even in our time, people are still attracted to a church where they hear the praises of God sung enthusiastically. Have you a singing faith?

John Wesley also believed in the redemptive approach to the vexing problems of his day. He believed that there could be no lasting reform apart from spiritually changed and redeemed men. It has been said that you cannot tie the ends of civilization together with ropes of sand. Jacob Riis, who labored in the slums of New York City a generation ago, once said that it was one thing to get a man out of the slums, and quite another thing to get the slums out of the man! We might well bear that caution in mind in our present war on poverty here in the United States of America.

Suppose that John Wesley were living in the England of this day; that he could observe modern England on a gambling spree so serious, that even her legal profession is greatly concerned. Suppose he could see her youth in a

[4] *Journal,* March 31, 1762.

state of moral anarchy, and observe less than 10% of her people attending church with any consistency. Suppose that he could see the moral turmoil right here in America, for certainly we are in no position to boast. Personally, I believe that John Wesley would adopt the same strategy he did in the past. It would be evangelism, yes, but suited and adapted to the needs of our day. He would insist that along with reform there must go the regeneration of men's hearts and lives. You just don't reform human beings en masse! You begin, if reformation is to be lasting, with the minds and hearts of men.

Wesley abhorred the practice of human slavery, whether in his own land or elsewhere, and worked hand in hand with William Wilberforce for its abolition. Six days before his death he wrote to Wilberforce: "Unless God has raised you up for this very thing, you will be worn out by the opposition of men and devils. But if God be for you, who could be against you. Oh, be not weary in well doing. Go on, in the name of God and in the power of His might, till even American slavery, the vilest that ever saw the sun, shall vanish before it."[5]

Believe me, this was no cloister religion, this religion of John Wesley!

Perhaps the crowning glory of Wesley lies in the fact that he had Heaven in his heart! Like St. Paul, he had his Romans, Chapter 8, and knew that nothing could separate him from God's love in Christ. The Kingdom of Heaven was joy in the Holy Spirit, already here and now.

Utterly self-giving and committed to the Christian cause, physically so frail that his health and life were often despaired of — still he kept on his appointed watch, until he was 88 years old.

If you, who read these words, are frail in body and

[5] Quoted by Paul S. Rees, *Things Unshakable* (Grand Rapids, Mich.: Wm. B. Eerdmans Pub. Co., 1947), p. 118.

anxious in heart, and would lay hold on the secret of Wesley, you would do well to attend to this prayer of his:

> Oh God, whose eternal Providence has embarked our souls in the ship of our bodies, prevent us from anchoring in any sea of this world, but help us to steer directly through it to Thy glorious Kingdom.

Toward the end of his days, he came on his last preaching trip to the town of Newcastle. The day was beautiful. All nature was in bloom. He said that if he did not believe in another world, he would want to spend the remainder of his days in this location. But he kept reminding himself that he was a seeker of another country, that here was not his rest.[6] The "joy of heaven to earth come down" that had accompanied him during his long ministry was calling him home.

Yes, he sought the city "that hath foundations," and finally entered it with a shout of victory. But not until he had left for us that last rapturous utterance of his: "The best of all is that God is with us." And so, the heart once strangely warmed entered the eternal glory!

[6] *Journal,* June 3 and 4, 1790.